web-empowered ministry

connecting with people
through websites, social media, and more

mark m. stephenson

ABINGDON PRESS
Nashville

WEB-EMPOWERED MINISTRY:
CONNECTING WITH PEOPLE THROUGH WEBSITES, SOCIAL MEDIA, AND MORE

Copyright © 2011 Mark Stephenson

All rights reserved.
No part of this work may be reproduced or transmitted in any form or by any means, electronic or mechanical, including photocopying and recording, or by any information storage or retrieval system, except as may be expressly permitted by the 1976 Copyright Act, the 1998 Digital Millennium Copyright Act, or in writing from the publisher. Requests for permission should be addressed to permissions@abingdonpress.com or to Abingdon Press, 201 Eighth Avenue South, P.O. Box 801, Nashville, TN 37202-0801.

This book is printed on acid-free paper.

Library of Congress Cataloging-in-Publication Data

Stephenson, Mark Morgan, 1960-
  Web-empowered ministry : connecting with people through websites, social media, and more / Mark M. Stephenson.
    p. cm.
  Includes bibliographical references and index.
  ISBN 978-1-4267-1322-4 (trade pbk. : alk. paper)
  1. Internet in church work. I. Title.
  BR99.74.S75 2011
  253.0285'4678—dc22

2010045754

11 12 13 14 15 16 17 18 19 20—10 09 08 07 06 05 04 03 02 01

MANUFACTURED IN THE UNITED STATES OF AMERICA

To the innovators and risk takers
around the world who maximize
the gifts God has given them
to take us all to new levels

Contents

Gratitudes

I am indebted to many people who helped make this book and my life in ministry possible:

I thank my parents, Ralph and Caryl Stephenson, for always believing I could do absolutely anything.

I thank my family—my wife, Ellen; sons Thomas, Andrew, and Michael; and daughter Mya—for allowing me to pursue this incredible adventure in ministry.

I thank Ginghamsburg Church pastor Mike Slaughter, staff, and lay leaders for creating an environment where ordinary followers of Jesus expect to do the extraordinary by the power of the Holy Spirit.

I thank the Ginghamsburg internet members Karen Smith and Chris Boerger—for dealing with the challenges I often cause and for working tirelessly to reach and serve others via the web.

I thank the Ginghamsburg unpaid servants Kate Johnsen, Deanna Bishop, Scott Berlon, and many more for devoting their time and talents to serving and making our church internet ministry what it is today.

I thank my colleague, Dr. Warren Bird, for encouraging me, teaching me, and helping me get my first book started.

I thank the current and future Web-Empowered Church Team—John Ward, Dave Slayback, Jeff Segars, Christoph Koehler, Dr. Bill Tenny-Brittian, Ben Fang, Glenn Kelley, Keith Hering, and others—for their technical expertise and willingness to serve churches around the world.

I thank the TYPO3 Community, all of them, from around the world, for sharing their skills and time to create such a powerful enterprise-class content management system.

Introduction

Do the God Thing

Perhaps my journey into internet ministry will help you see how God is working in your journey. I am an electrical engineer by training and have worked for several years in computer-related research, largely for the United States Air Force. When I came to Ginghamsburg Church, it did not even have a website; and it was not in a hurry to get one. Since my wife and I were new to the church, we attended membership classes where we took a test to help identify our gifts. The goal was to help us connect with a servant opportunity that fit our God-given gifts. The leaders told us that if we connected to the right ministry, then we would naturally enjoy it and draw energy from it. The problem was that the available opportunities did not fit me. After additional thought and prayer, I felt that I needed to start an internet ministry. Now that would energize me! Internet ministry has at times been very tough; the hours have been long, and it has been frustrating. However, since this ministry is my passion, I continue to love it, to draw energy from it, and to be blessed to serve in this unique way.

I encourage you to "do the God thing." I don't just mean do a good thing for God—any good thing—but instead get involved with a ministry about which you are passionate and for which God has gifted you. Just the fact that you are reading the beginning of this book is a sign that internet ministry may be your God thing.

Doing the God thing can be intimidating at times, but it is a real blessing to serve and be used by God for a divine purpose. As I continued to work to grow the ministry, my pastor, Michael Slaughter, told several of us he felt God telling him that our church would minister to ten thousand people by the year 2000. We realized that God was going to meet this goal in a nontraditional way because we had neither the space at the church nor the local population to achieve this goal through traditional church attendance. Instead, God allowed us to minister to many thousands of people through our web ministry. It is impossible to know exactly how many different people our web ministry has served, but all indications are that we met this ambitious God-sized goal right on schedule. God said it and it happened just as God said, because we did the God thing as best we knew how.

If internet ministry is your God thing, then I encourage you to just do it. You may or may not have the full support of leadership. For me, the support from our leadership started modestly but grew stronger as we all learned more about the ministry potential of the internet. From my discussions with other would-be internet ministry leaders, it appears that few organizational leaders are ready to jump into internet ministry. Many have limited understanding of this type of ministry, and many are what my friend Kate calls "TechNo"—when it comes to technology, they know nothing and are intimidated by it. Starting or expanding an internet ministry often begins with an education process. It's a little bit scary and a little bit different, but we need to go forward because the potential ministry impact is huge.

An internet ministry can also be good stewardship of your gifts, time, and resources. For example, pastors often spend many hours studying and prayerfully crafting sermons. These sermons are shared with a portion of the congregation on a given weekend (since not everyone shows up every weekend). By using the internet, you can make the sermon available to others both inside and outside of the congregation, now and in the future. People have sent us emails stating that content on the church's website has changed their lives. Many times, these people live hundreds of miles away, and the content they reference is months or even years old. Without the internet, they probably would not have experienced this benefit. And we are blessed to be able to share the gifts God has given us. We estimate that twice as many people will experience our church's sermons online versus in person. Web ministry multiplied the ministry impact of sermons by a factor of three. It is a blessing to do the God thing and to see the resulting fruits from our efforts.

The following chapters of this book are designed to help guide you on your unique journey toward building a powerful internet ministry. You will learn the practical steps, techniques, and ideas needed to develop an excellent and effective web ministry, and learn how to apply the many tools the internet has to offer, including websites, smart phones, social networking, media, instant messaging, and more to extend and multiply your ministry impact. People are coming to know Jesus. Lives are being transformed. It comes from God's power and churches' use of the internet to share, teach, and connect. It comes from doing the God thing.

CHAPTER 1

Getting Started

Getting past the excuses and setting out to web empower your mission

Wow! I am excited! A website opens up so many possibilities for our church. And, as a person who loves to play with computers, I can't imagine anything more fun than doing computer stuff for the Kingdom. It is a match made in heaven. This is going to be awesome!

With these thoughts in mind, I practically skipped into the office of the director of communications at our church to tell him my exciting plans for creating an internet ministry for our church. He told me that although it sounded interesting, someone else had already been working on it, and he suggested that I might be able to help after that person got it started. I needed to wait, which was not fun, but at least I knew I would still get to work on the website. So I waited for a few months and exchanged emails now and then to monitor the apparent lack of progress. I also took that time to learn more about building church websites because I really had no clue how to do it. I had never even created a webpage. After I sent multiple emails and made a couple more visits, it became clear to me that having a church website was far from a priority at our church. After all, our church had been around for more than one hundred years without a website. Although our communications ministry did not come out and say it, the feeling was that although a website is a good thing, other ministries are much more important. To me, the future possibilities for web ministry seemed endless and had the potential to amplify the impact of most all the other ministries in the church. To our communications ministry, at best, a website was good as long as it did not take significant time away from the other ministry activities.

I prayed often and continued reading and learning. Then I did something that might not serve as wise advice for you. I decided to build our website myself, without any help from the church. I found a church brochure and typed it into my computer. I scanned the church logo from the brochure and spent hours trying to doctor it up so it didn't look like I scanned it from the brochure. For that time and my skill level, the website looked OK, though I'd be embarrassed to show it to you now. I then met again with the director of communications. I told him I had created the initial website on my own and was about to register Ginghamsburg.org and post the website. I needed to know if the church was with me. The good news is that he chose to be with me and, in fact, helped me build a team to start the CyberMinistry. Neither of us knew the impact our website would have. Over the years, our church has become increasingly web empowered and has expanded to use additional web technologies (podcasting, blogging, social networking, instant messaging, phone apps, and so on) to the point that few ministry activities happen without some sort of web component. We are a web-empowered church and would not think of doing church any other way.

Perhaps you feel the same as I once did. You may be a pastor, a staff member, or (like I was) an unpaid church attendee attempting to help and serve. You see the critical need and amazing potential for web ministry, yet the decision makers, partners, and content providers see it as low priority or even a hassle. From my experience, I have learned that most of these people are busy with important ministry activities they understand well and that their knowledge of internet ministry is limited. This is a difficult combination to overcome. They might even be tech savvy and skilled internet users, but doing ministry with web technology is foreign to them. As one pastor told me, "They don't teach this stuff in seminary." And that is probably true for most pastors today. So, first, it is important to help educate your future partners in web ministry on this exciting opportunity to expand your ministry impact. Second, it is vital to be prayerfully and respectfully persistent. Unlike many other ministries, internet ministry is not easily accepted by everyone. Most other ministries in the church have been around for hundreds of years. Using the internet to expand and conduct ministry is often new and unknown, or even scary. But we must persist, even when we are not understood or fully supported. Please don't let naysayers stop you. The opportunity is too important. And it is really fun, too.

Internet Ministry Power

The internet is a powerful communications tool that you can use to dramatically increase the impact of your ministries. As you will learn throughout this book, most of the ministries in your church can be web empowered in some way to improve effectiveness and efficiency. With the internet, you can:

1. improve your church's communication quickly, easily, and inexpensively;
2. empower lay volunteers for active participation;
3. minister to people at any time and in any place;
4. connect people in caring community;
5. allow your sermons, devotions, and Bible studies to continue to minister for years to come; and
6. expand your ministry to reach people around the world.

It is time for us to fully harness the power of the internet for the kingdom of God. The result is likely to exceed your expectations and maybe mine, too. For example, we decided to put our church's sermons online. We began by recording, transcribing, editing, and then posting the sermon text and presentation graphics on our church website. Some months later, we were reviewing the website statistics provided by our hosting company. Among other things, website statistics can show the location of the internet service providers for the people who browse a website. As we examined the statistics, we were surprised to see that people were viewing our sermons from most every state in the union and from approximately twenty-five other countries. Wow, what a God moment! This surprise gave us our first glimpse of what might be possible through internet ministry. Now we commonly get visitors from more than eighty different countries each month, and thousands of people view our sermons each week. In fact, we estimate that more people view our sermons online than the 4,000-plus who hear them at our church each week. The web has allowed a church located in a rural, hundred-acre cornfield in Tipp City, Ohio, to minister to thousands of people all around the world. The same ministry power of the internet is available to your organization as well.

This book is based mainly on our church's practical experiences with the initiation and development of the main Ginghamsburg Church website (www.Ginghamsburg.org) and a few smaller websites created for our other ministries. Our main website went online in January 1997. The website continues to grow several pages every day. Most of the size is due to our posting online sermons, devotions, and Bible studies. The website also includes multiple years' worth of weekly sermons in video and audio format. Now the entire website occupies more than eighty gigabytes of disk space and receives more than fifty thousand visits each month. We also have many visitors who receive emails and text messages from our internet ministry. These statistics make Ginghamsburg.org one of the more visited "local church" websites in the world.

4

In this book, I'd like to share with you some of what we on the CyberMinistry team at Ginghamsburg have learned on our journey to create this exciting ministry, and also while working with other exciting web ministries around the world. You may be feeling intimidated or overwhelmed, but this book is made for organizations with limited time, limited funds, and limited experience. That's where we came from, too. When our CyberMinistry started, we weren't professional web developers. We were unpaid church attendees with busy lives and full-time non-web-related day jobs. We didn't hire a company or consultant to help us. When our website went live, our church budget for this ministry was about $25 per month. We learned on our own, making plenty of mistakes along the way. Even with the mistakes, we created a powerful internet ministry; you can create one, too.

Ten Excuses for Why Organizations Don't Have Web Ministries

Even as the internet has grown in popularity and importance in daily life, many churches and other Christian organizations remain hesitant to start a real internet ministry. Fortunately, most organizations now understand the need for at least an informational website. That is helpful, but it is a bit like driving a car around and never taking it out of first gear. It helps some, but it is far from utilizing its full potential. Below are ten common reasons cited for not having a web ministry. Each excuse includes a response that may be helpful to you as you advocate for and educate the organization's leaders about internet ministry.

1. We Don't Need to Do Ministry Online.

It is correct that our churches and Christian organizations do not need web ministries to function. But they do need web ministries to be more effective and to reach more people, which we all should want to do according to our missions and capabilities. God has allowed us access to this powerful communication tool, so we should apply it appropriately to enhance our mission. Just as Jesus stood in a boat or on a hillside to help people see and hear him better, we should use available resources to help others see God and hear God speak and minister through our organizations.

Also, since the internet has become an integral part of life for many people, they now expect organizations to have websites. In most cases, not having at least a simple website is like not listing your organization in the telephone book or not having a sign in front of your building. We commonly hear from people whose first exposure to our church was through our church's website. More people every day look to the internet as their primary source of all information, and that includes looking for a church. Your website is quite likely the first view people will have of your organization and should give them a taste of what they can expect when they visit.

Here is one example: A husband and wife were making plans to move to Ohio. As they searched the web for information on communities and churches, they found our church website. Based on the information and features on our website, they made the decision to move into our area just so they could attend our church. We assumed that they initially read the basic information about our church that should be on any church website—location, worship times, pastor's biography, and so on. But they told us that, instead of these, they began looking at our ministry features. They began viewing our video sermons each week and digging deeper. They also saw event information, prayer requests, Bible studies, and daily devotions. By the time they arrived at the door of our church, many of the common barriers that newcomers face in assimilating into the church were gone. Participating in our church online made them feel as though they had already attended our church even before they arrived in our area. It was the online ministry that ministered to them and led them to attend in person.

2. The Internet Is Filled with Sin.

For many people, the issue is fear of the unknown and the dark side of the internet. Through newspapers and television, we hear of an internet filled with pornography, hate groups, computer viruses, spam, and scams. Sin abounds on the public internet just as it does in other forms of public communication. The sin and evil found on the internet are all the more reason for every church to have a website. Jesus hung out with those who sinned and who did not believe. Each church should be where the needy people are found. We want our web ministry to be right in the midst of the sin-filled websites that we hear about. For example, we want our church webpages intermingled with links to the sin-filled webpages because people who go to an internet search engine looking for meaning or answers or fun will perhaps click our website link instead of others. We ought to be where people in need are, and many of them are on the internet.

3. It's Just Not Our Thing.

Clearly, not every church is called to produce a huge, fully web-empowered online ministry. Some organizations are called to transport hundreds of children to church in a bus ministry; others to set up a large shelter for the homeless; others to set up mission trips; and others to help young, unwed mothers. Different organizations are called to different missions based on their gifts and resources as well as the people they serve. I conducted web-ministry training in North Carolina, and afterward a pastor came up to me. He told me they have no indoor bathroom at his church and only recently got electricity to their building. Based on his situation and the people he serves, we both agreed that the bathroom was far more important than a website at this point. I was also blessed to correspond via email with a pastor in Africa. None of the people he serves have a computer or internet access. But, in my view, his ministry is web empowered. He has internet access and uses the internet to learn and grow in Bible knowledge and leadership. He also uses the internet to communicate with mission groups who come to his community to serve. These situations are less common circumstances for those reading this book; however, they do illustrate and remind us that we should use internet features when and where they fit. For most of you, a website is essential, and a web ministry is valuable.

4. We Can't Keep the Website Up-to-Date.

Far too often, I hear things like, "We created our website a long time ago, but it is totally out of date and we don't look at it," or "The person who built the website left the church and we can't even change it." I have literally seen Christmas Eve announcements on church websites many months after Christmas. Not good. Unfortunately, if the website is online, people have probably looked at it; and they may have been turned off or misled by it. The only thing worse than not having a church website is having a website that is obviously out of date. An incorrect website is not only misleading, it is a negative reflection on your organization. One key point to remember when creating a web ministry is that a web ministry is not a project to be completed. Instead, it is an ongoing ministry that requires attention and commitment—just like other forms of communication and other ministries. If your website is not up-to-date, then your organization is missing a ministry opportunity. And ministry opportunities matter to us, to those we serve, and to God.

5. The Internet Is Only for the Rich.

Certainly there is a cost to owning a computer and to having internet access. More and more people have internet access at home, at work, or in public facilities such as libraries, but it is unlikely that everyone you serve has access, and some of those who do have access may have poorly equipped computers or slow internet connections. To help people without internet access, we added kiosks at the church so people can visit our website there. Perhaps a ministry opportunity exists in your organization to equip and train people to use computers and the internet.

In any case, it is wise to make important information available in both electronic and nonelectronic formats. This allows people without easy internet access or people who prefer or need paper versions to receive the information. For example, our church has offered our newsletter in both electronic format (by email) and paper format. We asked that people volunteer to receive only the electronic copy; otherwise, they received a paper copy.

6. It's Too Expensive to Maintain a Web Ministry.

Of all the ministries in the church, an internet ministry is usually one of the most cost effective. The internet gives your organization access to the world. The potential of internet ministry is huge. To have a web ministry, you don't need expensive internet connections or the latest computers. You may be able to use free services for some features, host your website for free or at a reduced rate with a local hosting company, or use your denomination's hosting services. Otherwise, for most organizations, you can usually purchase hosting from a web hosting company for less than $30 per month. In most cases, the computers and internet connection you have access to are sufficient to create a web ministry. Internet ministry is worth the modest cost, and it can save money in reduced printing and mailing costs. In fact, our church can host its website for a year for less than the cost of one major printing and the postage to mail it. Finally, before you halt efforts to create an internet ministry because your leadership is taking a long time to approve its funding, please consider funding it yourself or in partnership with others who know the possibilities. Before you let cost stop you, please consider the cost to your ministry impact.

7. We Don't Have Anyone with the Skills.

People with computer skills and interests have traditionally had few opportunities to use their gifts and passions for ministry. It is likely that you have at least one person with the technical skills or interest to develop a web ministry. If so, this offers her or him a great opportunity for service. It happened with me, and I am forever blessed by this opportunity. In addition, the technical barriers are coming down as more powerful tools and instructional resources become available. When I started in web ministry, we had to manually create web pages in HTML. Now we have nice editors that allow us to easily update web content. I will talk more about these technologies in later chapters. In addition, with this book you are reading now (in paper or electronic form) you have instruction to help you develop the skills you need to build an active and productive internet ministry. You also have access to online communities to share and discuss internet ministry. In short, you and your team can do this and do this well.

8. Online Ministry Keeps People Away from Church.

Internet ministry, television ministry, and radio ministry have been criticized for encouraging people not to participate in a physical church where they can worship, have fellowship, and serve together in community. God designed us as social creatures with a need for other people, and a full Christian life includes relationships with fellow believers. We have talked with many of our website visitors, and most tell us that the website augments their Christian growth and does not replace church participation. We also know people who can't access church any other way, such as those who have physical impairments that make it impossible to travel or illnesses that make public contact dangerous, those who lack transportation, those who are out of town, and those who can't travel when weather conditions make travel unsafe. For these people an online option keeps them connected to church when they need it the most. In any case, an internet ministry should teach and encourage physical participation in Christian community and in service. An internet ministry does not and will not replace the importance of a physical Christian community. The internet cannot think, love, or physically hug. But, if it is done well, a successful internet ministry enables a church to be more effective and results in even more opportunities to interact in a personal way.

9. Technology Is Cold and Impersonal.

When telephone answering machines first became available, many people disliked them and would not leave messages. They would say, "I'm not going to talk to a dumb machine." Now the response to these devices is quite different. We receive long, detailed messages that sometimes don't even require us to call back. The fundamental capabilities provided by answering machines, now implemented as voice mail, are the same. So what changed? People adapted to this new form of communication. God designed us to be incredibly adaptive creatures, capable of maximizing the effectiveness of any communication technology. New communication technologies often feel cold and impersonal until we adapt to them. Email and instant messaging seem quite strange and even unusable to new users until they adapt. But for many people, once they become familiar with the technology, the messages almost shoot off their fingers into cyberspace. Before email and text messaging, you could never have convinced me that I would prefer to type rather than to talk; however, I now often choose email or text messages instead of the telephone for a variety of reasons. For example, with text messaging I can be in frequent conversation with my wife as I travel. Calls at each stop would become disruptive, but a simple text message is comforting and keeps us connected. And a text message that says "I love you" feels and is real. Communication technology that connects people does not stay cold or impersonal for long. God designed us to connect.

10. It Is Too Time Consuming.

Like most things that make a difference, internet ministry takes significant time and effort. I don't know of any ministry that is both powerfully effective and extremely easy to implement. But this book should help by allowing you to focus on creating and growing the ministry instead of spending time figuring out what to do. A major benefit and somewhat unique feature of this ministry is that it can be done from anywhere there is internet access, and it can also be done at any time. It is a ministry that is well suited for busy people and people who are free to work only at odd hours, or people who have a difficult time traveling. In fact, I still work from home even though I lead the web ministry at our church and the Web-Empowered Church ministry. Our web team members use their home computers and internet, work on the website when they can fit in the time, communicate most details by email or instant message, and meet in person occasionally just to talk.

Perhaps the Web-Empowered Church Can Help

The good news is that you are not alone in this internet ministry adventure. You have the option of getting assistance from a ministry I lead called Web-Empowered Church (WEC). (See WebEmpoweredChurch.org for more information.) WEC is a ministry of the Christian Technology Ministries International (CTMI), a nonprofit 501(c)(3) organization. The mission of WEC is to innovatively apply *web* technology to *empower* the worldwide *church* for ministry. The book you are reading, WEC online teaching, and WEC community forums all provide support to organizations that are building web ministries. Most important, WEC provides powerful, open-source web software that you can use for your church or Christian ministry website. And the WEC software costs you nothing. The WEC software runs on a web server on the public internet, and it allows you to create and maintain your website with powerful ministry features. The software has special webpages that allow you to create your website from a standard web browser (like Internet Explorer or Firefox) on your computer. No special software is required on your computer. With a proper username and password, you can make updates to your website from any computer connected to the internet. In fact, multiple people from your organization can help maintain your website.

The WEC software uses a free content management system (CMS) called TYPO3. TYPO3 does all the work of storing the content, creating appearance, and maintaining functionality of your webpages. Based on information you enter, the CMS automatically generates the webpages for people visiting your website.

You do not need to use WEC to benefit from this book because this book is about web ministry, not a specific tool; however, I will share more about the features of TYPO3 and WEC throughout the following chapters because I am most familiar with it, and it is specifically designed to web empower any ministry.

CHAPTER 2

Building a Team

Bringing the skills and gifts together to succeed

OK, let's get started. We've got the go-ahead to get our internet ministry going, but it seems like we need more people. There are so many things to do: the technical stuff to figure out, the graphic design (not my gift for sure), the navigation/organization, the photos, and the content writing. This requires diverse skills and knowledge. I don't have all of the skills and knowledge, nor do I have the time to do all of this.

We got some cookies and punch, put an ad in the church bulletin, and invited people to come after church to a meeting where they could learn about and join our new internet ministry. I waited in the room, praying that God would send someone. People began to arrive. Then more people arrived. We quickly opened the room divider to expand the room and hurried to get more chairs. The cookies and punch were gone in seconds. The stress of it all probably blotted out my memory, but I think there were about fifty people there. It felt like thousands. Once the group was seated, we talked about what we wanted to do with our church's newborn internet ministry. Because the turnout was much better than we had expected, we were not sure what to do with all the people. We got a list of their names and email addresses, thanked them for coming, and ended the meeting quickly.

The good news is that internet ministry intrigues people, many of whom will at least come to a meeting to check it out. The challenge is that you need to be ready for them when they come. We were not ready, but the one thing we had totally right was a desire to do internet ministry with a team.

The Secret to an Excellent Internet Ministry

I believe that the success our church has seen with our web ministry has little to do with technology and everything to do with team-based ministry. Beginning or growing an effective internet ministry should start by building a team that can carry out the many diverse tasks that such a ministry entails. An effective and sustained internet ministry requires teamwork for two main reasons. First, growing and maintaining the website takes a lot of time—people must gather, create, organize, edit, and post the content. And, people must research technical details and implement solutions. Second, internet ministry requires many different skills and gifts, and God does not stuff all these gifts into one person. God created us to be interdependent.

One result of not having a complete and effective team is a web ministry that starts with a flurry of activity, generates some webpages (even great webpages), and then goes dormant. The result is a common website phenomenon: the webpages have not been updated for months. The website says, "Come to our Easter Services," but it is October. Without an effective team, the ministry can lose momentum as members tire because they are overworked or are working outside of their passion, gifts, and interests. Beginning with a strong team is the best way to get started and the best way to keep the ministry going for the long haul.

In addition to starting with a team, it is important to remember that this activity is an "internet ministry" and not "website development." The word *development* implies a project that can be completed. A web ministry is never complete, just like children's ministry and worship are never complete. The word *ministry* implies an ongoing activity. We are never done with ministry. A web ministry is a living, changing, and evolving thing. New content must be added and updated, and web possibilities are always changing. For example, when we started our web ministry, there was no such thing as Facebook, YouTube, or Twitter. It takes a team to keep up with technology and to keep it alive and fresh.

If you have the funds, adding a web development company or paid staff to your team can accelerate the process, but it is not required. In the beginning, most budgets are not ready to support the added cost, and even very small organizations can usually create an internet ministry team from within. If you prefer, only low-level staff involvement is needed. We built our team of unpaid volunteers, called "unpaid servants," and created our first one thousand webpages before any paid person created a single page for our website. After the ministry got too busy, I transitioned from unpaid CyberMinistry team leader to paid director of CyberMinistry. And even then, I worked just one day per week for the church.

As our church became increasingly web empowered, we added our first full-time web staff person dedicated to web ministry, and that is where we are today. However, the staff has the critical responsibility of keeping our laypeople tasked and supported. While paid staff may build many of our webpages (especially time-critical pages), training and equipping our lay ministry team remain key. Unpaid servants supply much of the people power that makes our ministry go. I encourage you to build your team with all or mostly unpaid servants. It saves money, but more important, it provides a unique opportunity for people to participate in a ministry that can reach the world. Serving together in a team as we serve others helps us all grow in Christ.

The Kinds of Gifts We Need

Getting the right skill/gift mix among members of the team is important. There is more to internet ministry than gathering up all the web-savvy people in your organization. In fact, you will probably find that the majority of your team does not need to be web savvy. An effective internet ministry team commonly includes the following roles.

Leader: A leader articulates vision, motivates the team, and establishes direction and priorities. The leader decides what is posted on the website and other web features. The leader does not need to be a computer whiz but does need to have an understanding and appreciation for the significance of internet ministry. Pastors or communications leaders may serve in this role.

Manager: A manager keeps track of the many details associated with carrying out this ministry. The manager assigns tasks, monitors progress, and keeps the team healthy and moving forward. The manager typically needs some technical skills to be able to support the technical tasks.

Content Manager: A content manager understands the content, can prompt others for information, and is in tune with the many activities going on. The content manager verifies the accuracy and quality of the content and gets update requests and content to the other members of the team. In many ways, this is the most challenging role on the team. The lead church administrator often fits in this role well, as he or she would be familiar with all of the various ministries of the church.

Moderator: Web ministry often enables visitors to post comments on the website, such as those made on a pastor's blog. A monitor checks for and responds to appropriateness of visitor posts and actions, facilitates the health of the online community, and makes sure the organization is responsive to needs and requests.

Writer and Editor: Writers and editors create the textual content and support the organization of the website. They are often forgotten on web teams, but without them the web ministry literally has nothing to offer or offers content that is of poor quality. Writers and editors can be part of other ministries but need to be able to commit time to the internet ministry team.

Designer: A designer or graphic artist creates the overall appearance and page layout of the website(s) as well as the graphics and photos. Designers may also serve as photographers and animators. A website is very visual, and the appearance of your website is the first thing visitors see, so it is a blessing to have someone with the gift of visual design on the team.

Media: A media worker creates, records, and edits audio and video for the web ministry. This job includes capturing, editing, formatting, and uploading audio or video so it can be played online. Adding media is optional, but it is a powerful way to communicate.

Content Entry: A content-entry worker creates and edits content on webpages. Content management systems have reduced the technical skills required for content entry to only basic computer skills. Most people who can use a computer can be taught to do content entry. Content entry also requires a visual eye for the look of the page and proofreading skills to make sure the additions or changes are correct.

Web Developer: A web developer creates the more advanced webpages and converts and reformats content. For example, a web developer would resize, crop, or slice up graphics. A developer must understand HyperText

Markup Language (HTML) and Cascading Style Sheets (CSS). (See chapter 6.) Sometimes a web developer will use a scripting language such as JavaScript. Web developers often work with designers to implement the appearance and function of a website.

Programmer: A programmer develops webpages that can perform dynamic functions, such as looking up information stored in a database and displaying it on a webpage. Programmers can also write software to automate various tasks. Most organizations do not need programmers unless they plan to create new web applications.

Server Manager: A server or network manager, often known as the "webmaster," manages the website computer. Depending on your web hosting options, the server manager has different specific duties. In general, the server manager configures, monitors, and backs up the server computer. This includes management of all the data and files on the computer as well as the software that performs functions such as serving webpages and email. Most organizations do not need a server manager because these services are provided automatically by web hosting companies.

A newer team may not need a media worker, programmer, or server manager, but the other roles are important from the start. Of course, the roles can be shared and mixed to match team members' skills, gifts, and time availability. On a smaller team, these functions may be combined into roles for two or three people, but as the team grows, the functions will spread among more people. In spite of my solo/rebellious/feeble/embarrassing initial attempt at internet ministry, our internet ministry team at Ginghamsburg Church began with three people with varied skill sets. The makeup of a team can vary substantially, but in general, an internet ministry team needs to have people who fulfill the roles listed above.

One note of caution: I have counseled with several churches that have chosen a young person to lead and create its website simply because that person understands internet technology. This has not always worked well. A young, tech-savvy person can be a great addition to the team but may not be the best choice for a leadership role. The website is a window into your organization, so it is important to ensure that the website properly represents the character of your organization. A team leader must be equipped to make decisions about the content of the website, which will accurately portray what the church represents.

Getting People on the Team

There are multiple ways to recruit new members for the team. There are no set rules, but we have tried several techniques. Some worked well; others did not.

First, as I described earlier, we tried the "bulletin blast" approach that resulted in a group of fifty excited people interested in becoming unpaid internet ministry servants. This did not work out well. We were not prepared for such a large group, and most of these people had no experience doing anything other than browsing the web. We learned that few were ready for the time commitment that internet ministry requires. We discovered that although many people were interested in the internet, most were not equipped to support the team. The key lesson we learned was that, especially for the more technical tasks, a significant part of internet ministry includes training the servants.

The next technique we tried was designed both to recruit and to train. Since the interest among people in the church seemed high but their technical skill level seemed low, we decided to offer a web development class during the normal Sunday school time. Our hope was that those who did well in the class would want to join our team. Putting together the thirteen-week class took a lot of work, but there were many participants. Again, we had filled a room with excited people. The class was a valuable service and a truly enjoyable experience. But it did not yield a single addition to our internet ministry team. When the class was over, everyone thanked us profusely for all they'd learned, but no one wanted to join the team. Since it takes a great deal of effort to put together a class that is not likely to result in more servants, our team no longer uses such classes as a recruiting technique.

Our church currently uses two methods of recruiting. First, we have a ministry within our church that helps people identify their unique gifts and get connected to other ministries within the church. This connection team sends us the names and contact information for people who are potentially a good fit for participation in our ministry. The CyberMinistry team also automated this process by creating an online servant catalog that helps people find the right place to serve. Second, our team uses bulletin announcements when we have a significant need for someone with a specific skill. For example, an announcement might read: "Sermon transcriptionist needed to help transcribe sermon audio into text format to support our internet ministry" or "Person knowledgeable in server-side scripting (PHP and MySQL) needed for our growing internet ministry." These two approaches tend to yield a higher percentage of people with a real desire and capability to serve.

Matching people to tasks works best when the match is based on individual gifts and passion. Look for what excites folks within this ministry, and allow them to serve there even if it requires extra effort or if other needs seem more urgent. For example, we ask people who love children's ministry to help maintain the children's section of the website. We ask a person who is very busy but gets up early each morning for devotion and prayer to monitor the daily devotional email and resend it if it does not work. His help in this role is invaluable to the team because he catches problems before most of us even wake up, but more important, he has an opportunity to serve in a ministry he is passionate about, even with his busy work schedule. We match people—those who enjoy working with video, participating in the motorcycle ministry, taking photographs at youth events, proofreading and editing, scheduling tasks, entering sermons, and more—to needs within our ministry. The collective benefit of us all working as a team, each operating within individual gifts and passions, is amazing.

Equipping and Training Team Members

We require everyone in our ministry to have a computer with internet access and to legally own the software we use. We do this to keep costs down and because it would be difficult to track and manage church-owned items as people transition in and out of this ministry. Most people who want to participate in an internet ministry already have a computer and internet access. We occasionally purchase unique, special-purpose items for people who are already actively participating on the team. For example, we purchased expensive video digitizing/editing software and a large dedicated hard drive for the team member who digitized our sermon video.

Since we ask people to provide their own software, we keep costs down. The content-entry people use Microsoft Word to extract the text from Word documents and a simple graphics editor to resize and crop images. Tools like OpenOffice can read and edit Microsoft Word files if a free solution is needed. The content-entry people enter the content for our website using a common web browser. Our more highly skilled web developers may occasionally use tools like Dreamweaver and Photoshop.

Once internet ministry servants have the tools in place they must be trained. Currently, mentoring is the most effective training method we have found. When a person joins the ministry, we identify a task that he or she can accomplish while working with a mentor, a team member who is more experienced at the task. The mentor usually starts with a brief meeting to show the new team member how to do the task on a computer. Over time, the mentor remains available via phone, email, or instant message to review the work and to answer questions. We have successfully mentored people with minimal computer skills, helping them become productive members of the team. And then they can teach others. The process is not easy, but it is a successful system for developing new talent and team relationships. We will work with any person who has the capability to learn and is willing to put forth the effort to become a significant contributor to the ministry. In addition, for online training, we often recommend the online classes provided by the Web-Empowered Church ministry. These are useful to teach how to use the WEC-TYPO3 software to create or update pages and content on our website(s).

The Team Culture of *We*

It is important to maintain a team culture dedicated to excellence. Those of us on the CyberMinistry team *are* a team, so we use the language of a team. We always say that *we* do things. We say, "*We* updated the . . . ," even if only one person made the change. *We* added a new feature. *We* messed up. *We, We, We.* There are very few of us who enhance or modify the website without another team member contributing in some way. Even the leader behaves and performs in the context of a healthy supportive team.

Also, we are God's instruments, giving God the credit. For this reason, it is very important to establish a culture of excellence. While we are far from perfect, God deserves only our best. This is why we do not post pages or content that do not meet our standards. We work with authors to make it right. We ask others to review and test our pages. We ask everyone on the team to be on the lookout for errors. It can be easy to make a mistake, so we need to look out for one another. And we have made some big mistakes over the years. For example, when our church changed worship celebration times, we forgot to update that information in all the places it appeared on the website. Someone drove more than one hundred miles to visit our church, and the worship service was over. Another time we replaced the front page of the website with a blank page and did not notice for hours. And many times we have made mistakes that have crashed the server.

Mistakes will happen. The key is to catch and fix errors as early as possible. As a rule, we immediately drop everything else to fix an error. And we work as a team: the errors and fixes are team errors and team fixes. *We* make the mistakes, and *we* fix them. This culture of excellence and teamwork makes mistakes less personal and less frequent.

Go, Team, Go!

Every step our team takes together is preceded, conducted, and concluded in prayer. Our internet ministry is to be a God thing, and we work to keep it that way. We commonly pray for personal needs within the team that are not specifically related to web ministry. When someone new comes to the team, we assume God has a purpose for him or her, although that purpose may not immediately be revealed. So we never rush to place a person. It is not about filling empty slots. We want the Lord to drive our ministries, and we merely go where God leads. When we are recruiting and incorporating people into the team, we are always looking for God's leading and God's timing. If we can't fill a slot, we continue to pray and ask God to send the right person or guide us to the right solution.

Meeting and praying together are also important. The frequency of our team meetings depends on the current projects and the influx of new team members. We don't need many meetings because we communicate regularly via the web. We communicate through standard email, instant message, and Skype (free voice over IP). Using these technologies, we are able to communicate as needed, sometimes multiple times per day for specific projects. We also enjoy sharing encouraging emails that we receive from those who visit our website(s). Even within a team, internet ministry can feel lonely now and then, and sometimes you wonder if anyone is out there in cyberspace. Personal emails are a great boost to the team, reminding us that this is about ministry, not technical stuff. We are ministering to real people who need Jesus and who need to grow in Christ. Their emails help us know that our efforts are reaping Kingdom benefits.

We also benefit from a monthly report summarizing the ministry activities. Each month we produce a report that is emailed to our senior staff leadership and to the internet ministry team. The monthly report is an excellent tool for educating the church leadership on the significance of our ministry. Most senior staff members do not have background and training in internet ministry, so this report helps them understand our ministry impact. In the report, we list the team members and summarize various features and statistics for each portion of our website. For example, we list the number of website visitors, online subscribers, prayer requests posted, and cell-group sign-ups. We include statistics from previous months so we can compare to the current month. Perhaps most important, we include copies of emails we have received from website visitors. These personal emails help our leadership and our team understand this ministry's impact on real people. Our church is also a teaching church, so we commonly exchange email with leaders of other church internet ministries, and these emails show the impact of our teaching ministry.

Of course, the real activity of internet ministry is not the meetings or the reports; it is the frequent additions and changes to the website(s). Most organizations will update their website at least once a week, and many (including us) make changes nearly every day. Keeping this process going can be a challenge. The church needs to make sure information is flowing to the team at the appropriate times. The team then needs to send web content to the appropriate team member who can prepare it and post it to the website(s), help team members if they have questions, review changes added by team members, work with team members if there are issues with their work, and post the changes. The only team members who are allowed to post to the website directly are those who are experienced and have demonstrated excellence.

As team leaders communicate with the team, we also work to support each team member emotionally and spiritually. Webpages can wait if we need to support a team member. Keeping our team healthy and strong is vital to the ongoing ministry, so we commonly exchange emails that have nothing to do with websites. We exchange prayer requests and general discussion about ordinary happenings. I keep a prayer list for team members and often pray for the team as a whole, individual team members, their families, and the ministry. Because the team can function as a small-cell group, we also visit team members and their loved ones in hospitals or comfort them at funerals. As you make more of a difference in a ministry, it often seems as though the enemy, or sin, seems to attack more. So it is vital to keep both yourself and the team emotionally and spiritually strong.

CHAPTER 3

Creating a Strategy

Defining the right approach, content, and features for your mission

It's time to build our website. I'm a high-technology kind of guy, and God really deserves something spectacular. I am determined to create the coolest, most high-tech church website in the world. We will have every technology trick in the book and a few more that we invent ourselves. We will include JavaScript, moving pictures, random pictures, mouseovers, dropdowns, pop-ups, scrolling text, XHTML, XML, RSS, SQL, PHP, CSS, and every other letter combination out there. The graphics are going to be spectacular. The buttons will look like shimmering gold, and the website will look like it is in three dimensions by including blending, shadows, shining, and reflections. When people see it, they will stand in awe.

I set out to build an award-winning church website with all the bells and whistles you can imagine. The initial version was a rather painful adventure that took ten times longer than expected, but I created something that started us down the web technology path. It looked pretty cool on my computer. I uploaded it to my website and headed for the church to show it off and (so I expected) to receive praise and expressions of awe from the staff. The painful lessons began as awe turned to awful. First, the front page took forever to load. Then, the pages would not fit on smaller monitors at the church. All the cool shading was converted to a huge mosaic of polygons, and the textured background looked horrible. And, to top it off, the scrolling text trick did not work with the browser the church used.

Over the years I have learned more about the use of graphics and technology. The bottom line is that great websites are not great because of spectacular designs or the latest technologies (even though those shimmering gold buttons looked pretty cool). People care most about what is between the HTML tags— the content! Appearance and technology are there to enhance the presentation of the content, but content is the key.

It's All About Content

Think about the websites you visit frequently. Why do you go there? People don't return to a website over and over because of the graphic design and the cool technology. Google is among the most visited websites in the world, and it does not look fancy—it is quite simple and rather boring. The draw to Google is that the user can rapidly and easily get a list of web links. We are drawn to Google because of the utility of the content it provides for us. Facebook is popular because we get to see comments from our friends, photos, and other social networking features. Our friends and connections to them matter to us, and that content draws us there. The websites we visit over and over are those that provide content we care about and features that we can and want to use. When I talk to people about a new web ministry, they often begin by saying they want technologies like a podcast, a blog, and text messaging. But these are content delivery mechanisms, not content. They may make a lot of sense if they are used to communicate the right content to the right audience; otherwise, they may not be helpful at all.

As we start to build an outstanding web ministry, our main focus should be on content. At Ginghamsburg Church, the most popular sections of our website are sermons, Bible studies, and devotionals. The majority of content that people really want is in these sections. Content can also come from interactive features such as our pastor's blog or our prayer page. But having the coolest blog technology around will not draw people unless our pastor posts to the blog regularly and those posts are of interest to the visitors. Even the interactive features are all about the content inside them even though the content may have multiple sources. You must consider the content first and then choose the appropriate delivery mechanisms for your visitors.

Who Is Your Target Web-Ministry Audience?

Content is key, but the content must be relevant to the visitor. A website may be filled with information, but if people don't care about that particular information, then they don't care about the website. The first step in deciding what content to add is deciding who forms your target web-ministry audience. Leaders in your organization who understand your mission and vision for ministry can best make this decision. They may do so by answering questions like *Who do we want coming to our website? Who are we speaking to? Who do we want to serve?* Your web ministry might serve some of the following groups: potential church attendees, current church attendees, church members, church leaders, other churches, pre-Christians, Christians, anti-Christians, children, youth, college students, senior adults, single parents, singles, married people, divorced people, depressed and lonely people, people who are blind, people who are deaf, artists, bikers, and more. You might say, "We want to serve them all." That would probably be impossible to do effectively with a single website. Most organizations would find it difficult even to generate the content needed to serve all these groups.

Let's say you want to create a web ministry to help children grow in Christ. Clearly this website will be different from one designed to reach isolated and lonely adults. The appearance, content, organization, and features will all be dramatically different for each of these target audiences. You need to choose a focus based on your organization's mission, gifts, and resources. Most initial church web ministries focus on adult potential church attendees, current church attendees, and church members. If you do choose to target people in vastly different groups, you should consider creating more than one website. But choosing a target audience is critical; otherwise some visitors to your website will be confused or poorly served.

Multisite churches, which are increasing in popularity, have some other challenges as well. They end up with multiple target audiences or at least multiple content elements that need to be different for different sites, while other content needs to be the same for all sites. Our Web-Empowered Church (WEC) software has a powerful feature that either can display identical content elements on multiple websites (if you change it in one place, it changes in all places) or can create one website that changes specific elements based on the site a user selects. For example, worship times could change based on the visitors' selection of church campus even though they are browsing just one website.

Our main Ginghamsburg Church website, for our multisite church, targets potential church attendees, church attendees, and church members. After the main website was up and running, we added a few more websites and the option to choose a site on our main website. One additional website supports youth ministry and focuses on outreach to youth in our community. As you would expect, each of these websites differs in appearance, content, organization, features, and website visitors. We also added a Facebook page and Twitter, which are mainly used for announcements and social connection.

What Are They Looking for from Your Web Ministry?

You have chosen the target audience(s) for your web ministry. The next step is to determine what they are looking for that you can provide. You may need to study your target audience(s) to better understand their needs; however, if you chose target audience(s) that you are already supporting, then you probably have a good sense of what they seek.

When some organizations start an internet ministry, there is a frantic push to put online all the information they can gather. The thought is that filling the website with content is good. This is not the best way to approach web content. In fact, it could even be disrespectful to your visitors. Wisely choose the information you post online. Adding extra information in which people are not interested only clutters up the website and makes it more difficult for visitors to find the information they want. Our mission is to serve people, and we can do so by providing relevant and concise information. As you work through this process, you are likely to find that you need to modify some existing written information as well as create some brand-new information. However the information is delivered (webpage, cell phone, blog, Facebook, and so on), the important thing is for the information to be something that website visitors desire or need.

The following exercise will help you to determine what content is appropriate for your target audience(s).

During one of the first meetings of the newly formed internet ministry team, hold a brainstorming session with a few leaders who serve in communications. On a whiteboard, write the target audience(s). As a group, talk about and list the kinds of things you would want if you were a member of your target audience(s). If your target audience is potential attendees, put yourself in the shoes of someone viewing a website for a church she or he has never seen before—one she or he might want to attend in the future. What should be on that website to help her or him decide whether or not to attend? You might list things such as directions to the church's location(s), what the church believes, its worship style, its music style, worship times, pastor's biography, activities for kids and for youth, classes for adults, special support groups, current activities, instructions for parking, instructions for dropping off a child, and so forth. Since this is a brainstorming session, you will eventually need to refine and organize the list, but once it is refined, this will become the initial list of content to gather or create for your website.

The next step, which can be done with the full group or a smaller group, is to go through each of the items on the list and discuss how to deliver the content to the visitor. For example, "music style" might require more than a text description. Perhaps there is a noncopyrighted song you could post in audio or video so people can really get a feel for what your music ministry is like. If you have special parking for visitors, think about including a map or a photo to help visitors find it. Some churches create an entire sequence of pages that walk through a first visit to the church, telling visitors where to go, what they will see, and what they will do. For potential attendees, the first visit to a church can be a very scary thing. Starting with a virtual visit can make it a lot easier for them.

As you work through how best to provide content to website visitors, consider active features that can assist your target audience. For example, you may want to add a discussion forum, an email newsletter, a blog, a calendar, a slideshow, registration forms, or a private area that requires a username and password. As with simple content, you should choose active features based on your target audience. There is more information on active features later in this book.

Go through the process of brainstorming, refining, and organizing the content list. Decide the best ways to share the information on the website. Choose active features. Do this for each target audience you plan to support. Notice that the information you need may not be the same as the information that already exists on paper. For example, you may not have included a picture of the visitor parking spaces in your print visitor information. The key is to gather the right information for the people you want to serve, and present it in a way that makes sense to them. Once you know what the right content is, you can mobilize your team to gather and create it—whether text descriptions, photographs, audio, or video—and the technical member(s) of your team can begin to work on the active features.

Now for a fun trivia question: excluding the front page and other pages made up of mostly links and minimal content, what has been the most-visited content page on the Ginghamsburg website? Most people are surprised at the answer. It is our pastor's biographical page. This is something we didn't anticipate. Perhaps this is because our pastor is well known, or perhaps it is because we have links to that page in several places. In any case, it seems reasonable to expect that people will want to know about the pastor of the church. A church website should include biographies of your pastor and each of the main church staff.

The Words We Use

In addition to choosing the right content for the audience, internet ministry teams need to choose the right words—ones that people can fully understand. Christian organizations have a unique religious language. We use words such as *justification, sanctification, edification, sacrament,* and *holy.* These words may be unfamiliar or even intimidating for our target audience. Even the more common words such as *prayer, communion,* and *sermon* may be unfamiliar or may hold differing connotations for visitors with varied backgrounds. Especially in the more general and introductory portions of your website, use easily understandable terms or provide extra explanation to facilitate understanding. For example, instead of simply saying "pray," use "speak to God through prayer" to provide additional explanation. Or you could refer to a "sermon" as the "pastor's message."

The preferred language depends on your target audience and the words you use. Church words are often important words for visitors and members to learn and understand at some point, but think carefully about when these words should be introduced, and start with words that the people you are serving are likely to understand without difficulty or confusion.

In addition, organizations often like to create their own home-grown names for things. For example, our church uses various nicknames for children's ministry spaces. Depending on the ages of the children, they go to "The Nursery," "The Tree House," "The Backyard," or "The Avenue." Classes can meet at the "MC," the "DC," or the "Arc." Within the church, these names are fun and come with a nice theme and logos, but to potential visitors, they may be confusing. Easy ways to clarify terms include adding words that help define them ("The Avenue youth ministry") and spelling out acronyms ("Discipleship Center [DC]").

With any given target audience, writing for the internet is different from writing for paper. People are not typically willing to sit in front of a computer for long periods of time to read large amounts of text. The subcultures of the internet are fast moving and to the point. People will read small blocks of potentially interesting text but quickly skip large blocks with a click of the mouse. So existing written information may need to be adapted before you place it on your website. If at all possible, keep sections of text short and to the point. When in doubt, use fewer words.

Some content, such as in an article or a sermon, requires more text. There are a few ways to make large blocks of text more likely to be read. You can break up the text with graphics, bulleted lists, and shorter paragraphs, or spread the text across a sequence of webpages instead of placing it all on one page. You can also provide a printable version. A printable version has the added feature of allowing people to save hard copies and share them with others.

Content Challenges

One tip to help your initial internet ministry days go more smoothly is to start your website with static content—content that is not changing all the time. For example, directions to your organization and a statement of beliefs probably do not change very often. In contrast, dynamic content is constantly changing and, therefore, much more difficult to keep up-to-date. An example of dynamic content is a calendar, which is best not posted at all if it cannot be kept up-to-date. Maintaining dynamic content makes it hard to build static pages because your team is frequently interrupted by the need to update the dynamic content. Dynamic content is best added when your team is well established and the organization is committed to supplying the content to keep it going.

Another tip is to make gathering content a high priority. The number one complaint we hear from people in internet ministry is that they are not able to get information to add it to the website or to keep it up-to-date. This can be frustrating for those responsible for the website and embarrassing for your organization as website visitors see inaccurate or incomplete information. Perhaps an administrative person who is really connected with all that is going on could be responsible for getting the latest content to the internet team or could be trained to make updates directly. At our church, we have had problems getting data from some ministry leaders for years. People who lead ministries tend to be busy people, and internet ministry is often the last thing on their overloaded to-do list. After years of frustration, we decided to change things. We still request information, but we post only what people give us. The ministries that give us information have great webpages with lots of content. The ministries that do not give us information have a brief summary that we got from a previous brochure. As ministries see what is possible, they begin to want their section of the website to be better, and we receive more content.

Keeping It Legal

Internet ministry would be much easier if there were no copyright, trademark, or privacy laws, but we must abide by them for both legal and moral reasons. It is increasingly frustrating for us because of all the trademark violations, copyrighted material, and privacy violations we commonly see and hear on the internet on social media websites like YouTube and Facebook. It appears that enforcement is applied sporadically based on various lawsuits. Unfortunately, as of the time of this writing, these laws addressing social media are in their infancy. Watch for new developments as companies and the legal system try to adapt better to the internet. The best I can do now is to share about the current situation.

You may have a wonderful recording of a song you want to post on your website, but you can't legally do so unless (1) you own the lyrics and music, (2) you have written permission from the owner to use the material, or (3) the lyrics and music are in the public domain. The same is true for musical arrangements. Old hymns are typically OK to post because they tend to be in the public domain, but you cannot legally post them if copyrighted arrangements were used in their performance. You need permission to use both the words and the music. There are special licenses that you can purchase in order to sing lyrics and play music in church, but unfortunately, they typically do not apply to posting that same music publicly on the internet. Most music licenses have some limitation on the distribution, and the challenge with the internet is that it has almost infinite distribution potential. At our church we post video of our sermons; however, except for a few songs our band wrote and arranged themselves, we are not able to post the music even though we know it would be of great benefit. This becomes more complicated when a sermon incorporates a song or a person speaks while a copyrighted song is playing in the background. The effect of speaking over music can be powerful. So for those times, we ask that the musicians use noncopyrighted music. A small portion of a song, especially when a person cannot tell what song it might be, is allowed; otherwise, we must remove that section from the audio we post on the website.

One possible exception has occurred of late. Some churches are now implementing live or prerecorded online worship experiences that include copyrighted music. Their understanding is that this is allowed if the online events are restricted to specific times and not on demand, they count the number of online attendees, and they pay license fees based on the total attendance at both physical and online events. Essentially they are treating online worship events just like they treat physical worship events. This is an exciting potential opportunity if it remains legally acceptable.

Commercial video clips also have copyright issues. Portions of video clips from movies can be licensed for use inside a church worship service, but they are usually not allowed on the web at all, unless you can get written permission. And finding them on YouTube or a similar online video service does not make using them legal because they were probably posted there illegally. Experience has taught us that permission is either impossible to get or carries an outrageous cost. For this reason, we ask the pastor to summarize all clips from commercial movies or television before or after they play because the people who view sermons on the web will not be able to hear or see them. We remove all such clips from what we post online.

All website content is automatically copyrighted, even if there is no copyright notice on the website, so you need permission to copy content (text, graphics, audio, video, and so on) from another website. An email granting permission and specifying its use is usually sufficient. You do not need permission to link to another website. In fact, most websites appreciate the publicity because it increases their number of visitors and helps improve their search engine rankings.

Magazine and newspaper photos and other published material are typically copyrighted. You need to get written permission from the owner and possibly pay a fee to use them. You can purchase photos or graphics individually or in groups, which include permission in the license agreement for use on websites. There are also websites that claim to have royalty-free graphics, but it is difficult to know where they acquired all their images. It is important to read their license agreements to ensure you can use them freely on your website. Creating your own graphics is safest. Then you know who the owner is.

Original photos or video of noncopyrighted and nontrademarked items are generally OK to use on your website. If you take pictures of children, get written permission from their parents to use them on the web. It is good to have written permission from adults when using their images, as well. If you take pictures in public places where people cannot expect to have privacy, it is generally legal to post those pictures of adults. This is how the paparazzi can get away with selling public photos of celebrities. But we hold ourselves to higher standards, so even if it is legal, it may not be appropriate or respectful of others to use their picture or a video of them on the web. Determine your policy and stick to it.

Due to the various privacy laws and other issues, we often stage pictures that include only our staff or long-term members and their families. We sometimes modify the photos to remove people or to obscure their faces. If someone can't be recognized, then you do not need his or her permission to use the picture. If anyone requests to have their picture removed from our website, we remove it immediately even when we have the legal right to use it. There is no reason to let that conflict continue.

For additional privacy and protection, to avoid prank callers, and to avoid email spam, it is best to not post personal phone numbers, addresses, or email addresses on your website. We ask people to call the church to get phone numbers or addresses. We set up automatic forwards so that email sent to a church email address is automatically forwarded to the person's private email address.

These laws can be difficult to understand, but it is important for Christian organizations to follow them to avoid potential lawsuits and because we should obey the law and treat people respectfully. I am not a lawyer, and the information in this section should not be considered legal advice. Please consult a lawyer for the details regarding these issues.

Help Them Find It

You may have a great plan for identifying and generating the right content and features, but the content and features won't serve their purpose unless the website visitor can find them. Organizing the website is very important. Most visitors understand that websites are organized into sections, subsections, and pages. Organize the content similar to the hierarchical outline of a book with chapters, sections, and subsections. The organization criteria should be something your target audience can understand.

Here is a way to get started: First, list the name of each piece of content you are planning to have on your website (pastor's bio, forum, driving directions, and so on). Then, attempt to put the content elements into logical groups based on criteria that seem to make sense to your target audience. There should not be more than ten groups; five or six groups would be better. Once you are comfortable with the groups, they can become the major sections of your website. If you have many content elements in one group, consider splitting it into two groups or define subgroups.

Section names are important because they are key to a visitor having an idea of what is inside the section. Look at each group of content elements and attempt to name it with a word or a short phrase that the target audience will naturally understand. This can be very challenging, and there are no perfect answers.

Do the best you can. You may need to move content to a different group because it does not fit after you choose a section name. Avoid religious words and local church lingo. At Ginghamsburg, for example, we should not have a section named "The Avenue" (which only those who already regularly attend our church might understand), but a section called "Ministries," with a subsection called "Youth."

As you work through this process, you may feel the need to have sections, subsections, subsections of subsections, and so on. To simplify access to the website content, try to minimize the "depth" of the website. The "depth" refers to the number of mouse clicks visitors must make to get to the content they seek. Keeping the depth to less than five clicks is usually best, and important content should not be more than a couple mouse clicks away.

Here is an example of a website outline:

Home (front page)
About Us
 Services
 Directions
 What We Believe
 Our History
 Staff
News and Events
 Calendar
 News
Community
 Pastor's Blog
 Forum
 Prayer
 My Account
Ministries
 Adult
 Youth

Children
Missions
Worship
Learn and Grow
Sermons
Devotional
Classes

One option for choosing names is to make the section names action words, or verbs. Most visitors come to a website with a purpose. Action words more directly connect to the needs of the visitor. Here are some examples of verb-based section names: Worship with Us, Explore the Church, Meet Jesus, Grow in Christ, Connect with People, Serve Others, Get Support, and Nurture My Kids.

For popular pages that are a few mouse clicks into the website, you may want to create a "hot link." A "hot link" is a link, usually on the front page, that takes the visitor directly to a page inside the website. The page can be found through a sequence of mouse clicks, but the "hot link" bypasses all the normal navigation and takes the visitor straight to the page. A group of hot links on the front page is useful but not required.

Once you have a basic outline, test it. Pick a content need your visitors might have, and follow the process for finding that content. For example, imagine a visitor coming to the website for the first time. Imagine that this visitor has a thirteen-year-old son whom he or she wants involved in youth activities. Looking at the names of the sections and subsections, is this visitor likely to pick the right path through the website to get to the content he or she seeks? Identify and correct any potential points of confusion.

The Most Important Word on Your Website

The most important "word" on your website is your domain name because that is what visitors will type in and what other websites will link to. The domain name is the text that uniquely identifies your website among all other websites in the world, for example, YourChurchName.org. A domain name is treated the same whether written with upper- or lowercase characters (MYCHURCH.ORG = mychurch.org = MyChurch.org) so it may be helpful to mix the case to make it more readable. You may hear people refer to your web address as a "URL." This is a techie term that stands for "Uniform Resource Locator." The URL includes a prefix that helps the computers know how to communicate. A full URL has the format *http://www.Your ChurchName.org* although the *www.* is usually optional and is becoming less common. Like the other content on your website, the domain name should make sense to your target audience. You want a name that people can remember and are likely to type in correctly, so you should generally avoid acronyms or abbreviations unless you are confident people will remember them. Pick a name that describes your website. For a church website, using your church name is usually best. The challenge is that all domains on the internet must be unique, so you may need to get creative in order to find a unique name. Including the word *church* in your domain name is optional. Shorter names are generally better, but they are more likely to be taken already.

The letters in your domain after the dot ("dot" is web talk for the period) are called the top-level domain (TLD). The TLD is part of your unique domain name. YourChurchName.org is a different domain than YourChurchName.com or YourChurch Name.us. Examples of TLDs are "com," "org," "net," and "info." It is best to register domains with both "org" and "com" as the TLD. "Org" was designed for nonprofit organizations (like churches), and "com" was designed for companies. However, some people assume that "com" goes at the end of all domains, so it is wise to own both and to have either one take people to your website. There are no restrictions on who can register which TLDs, so it is fine for a church to register a "com" domain. The TLD can also be a country code. A country code is always two letters, and every country has a unique country code. The country code for the United States is "us." If "org" and "com" are not available for the domain you want to register, then you could use a country code. A few countries have interesting country codes with other meanings: Tuvalu has a country code of "tv," and Micronesia has a country code of "fm." Using a country code may cost more than other TLDs because the country to which they are assigned controls them, but it is OK to use them.

Since the domain name must be unique, it must be registered. The organization that manages all the domains is called the "Internet Corporation for Assigned Names and Numbers" (ICANN), www.icann.org. ICANN does not sell domains, but there are many vendors and hosting companies where you can purchase a unique domain name. The typical cost is about $15 per year, and you can choose to purchase multiple years. Domain name vendors are easy to find with a quick web search.

Here are four pointers I hope will help you in the process of establishing a domain:

1. Vendors often try to sell extras with your domain name, and it is unlikely that you will need anything except the domain name, so carefully skip past extra options you must pay for.

2. Many hosting companies will purchase the domain on your behalf. If you choose later to change hosting companies, then your hosting company is obligated to allow you to move even though it would be losing the ability to host your website.

3. Your domain will be added to the ICANN database by any vendor with whom you register a domain. Domain name vendors can make the process a little easier for you by creating nicer web-based registration tools, but no company will result in a better registration.

4. If you register at one domain name vendor, you can transfer your domain name to another vendor if you would like.

The process is not simple, but vendors are required to allow you to change.

Any vendor that offers domain names also has web forms that allow you to search for a new domain. You may see the term "whois" used to refer to searching in the database of registered domain names, which is sometimes called the "whois database." To find out if a domain is already registered, you type in the proposed domain and submit the form. I am always amazed at how many of the domains I attempt to find are already registered. Finding a unique domain name may take some patience. Just keep at it until you find one that will work for you.

Once you find a domain name that is not already registered, you can go through the registration process to purchase it and to enter its initial settings. You will be asked for contact information and for a list of each primary Domain Name System (DNS) or, simply, "Name Server." You can get this list from your hosting company. The names vary but may look a little like this: ns1.YourHostingCompany.net. There will probably be three or more of them, and you need to list them all. If you purchase your domain through your hosting company, then it should automatically set these values for you.

Domain names were created because people can remember text names more easily than they remember numbers; however, numbers work best for computers. The DNS does the translation from the letters in your domain name to a unique numeric identifier called an Internet Protocol (IP) address. The IP address is the unique number that corresponds to your web server on the internet. It is traditionally written down as four numbers (between 0 and 255) separated by dots. For example, 10.20.100.200. However, since so many IP addresses are now needed, you may end up with a new IP address that has eight four-digit hexidecimal numbers separated by colons. This very large number is called IPv6 and is four times longer than the older IPv4 format. Here is an example of an IPv6 IP address: 1010:2020:3030:4040:5050:A0A0:B0B0:C0C0.

A primary DNS is one of a small number of DNS computers on the public internet that are designated as the official source for your domain name and the corresponding IP address. The primary DNS computers then share that information with DNS computers around the internet so people can access your website. When you register your domain, you must supply the list of primary DNS computer addresses as a way to get your website known to the internet. In addition, your web hosting company must add your domain information (domain name and IP address) to the primary DNS computers so they can share the information. Once all this is done, it usually takes less than forty-eight hours for the entire internet to know about your new domain. In fact, some computers are likely to know about it in just a few minutes. It really is amazing how well and how quickly it usually works.

CHAPTER 4

Serving Your Visitors

Meeting the needs of the online people you serve

A mother wrote, "This ministry is a godsend for so many people. I know I'd personally be lost without it. Thanks for being there for me!"

A woman in Australia emails me when our text sermon postings are running behind. She reads them, prints them, and selects the right ones for several different people she knows. Her ministry is to select and share sermons with others.

A soldier emailed me because the military computers did not allow him to install our video player, so he could not watch our video sermons. That night, we began reencoding the video in a format that he could watch, and we have continued to do so ever since.

Another soldier, a military chaplain at a classified location, wrote, "I enjoy checking out your site as I use sermons from the internet as commentaries in preparing my own sermons here in the field."

One Sunday while visiting my wife's family in rural Indiana, we went to the worship service at a small country church. Afterward, I shook hands with the pastor and told him we were visiting from Ohio where we attend Ginghamsburg Church. He said that he visits the Ginghamsburg website all the time and, in fact, had used a couple of online sermons in preparation for the sermon I had just heard.

A woman in China pleaded with us to quickly fix a problem with our video sermons: "The sermons are a God lifeline for me. It is very difficult to get to the church in Shanghai, so we don't go very often. With the sermons being online, I can pull them up whenever I want to and listen to the messages. It's the next best thing to being in church."

A local TV news station interviewed a survival expert from our church who travels around the world, teaching soldiers how to survive if they get separated from their unit. On camera, he broke into tears as he talked about watching the sermons on our website in order to stay connected with the church and "to feel part of it again."

A man who is totally blind informed us that he browses our website all the time using a special program that reads the words on the page to him. Until he told us, we did not even know this was possible.

A church in Canada was without a pastor. Attendees had no one to preach on Sunday. They contacted us and got permission to use sermons from our website. They printed the sermons and had someone in their church read them from the pulpit to fill in for the Sunday sermon.

A small group of young pastors-in-training who live in Kenya meets each week to study the Bible together. The Bible study they use is often downloaded from the Ginghamsburg website.

A soldier stationed in South Korea writes, "I am currently leading a women's study here at Camp Stanley and have recently been using the Bible study from the online sermons for our discussions. Your website is amazing and is ministering all over the world!"

A man who consistently listens to our video sermons was waiting in the hospital where his son was having surgery. A fearful mother was waiting there too and began to ask questions about God. The man told me that her questions matched a recent sermon he had heard on our website. He led her to Christ by going through the main points from that sermon.

These are some of the more spectacular stories we have heard over several years of internet ministry. There is no way of knowing to whom your website will minister. We never imagined that any of these people in these circumstances would come to our website. But we now know one thing: if we had not stepped out in faith and added the content to our website, then all these people would have missed a blessing.

But How Do They Find the Website?

People find websites in many different ways, and it is often difficult to determine exactly how or why. We know that many times plain old-fashioned word of mouth or computer/internet-assisted word of mouth is key. The internet makes the world so connected that it is now common and easy to send an email to a friend that contains a link to your website. Blogs, Facebook and other social networking websites, online discussion groups, articles, and other websites may link to your website. They all help people find you.

The first place to expand the reach of your church's website is right in your organization. Once you have the website up and ready to go, you should include the web address on all your publications. Wherever you include the phone number or physical address, include the web address, too. Announce the web address and include it in the bulletin or newsletter. Add it to your business cards. Add it to your sign. I have seen a few churches that purchased a huge banner with their web address on it and hung the banner on the side of their church. Most passersby will never enter your church; however, some may type in the web address from the banner just to see what it is all about.

If your church has social networking accounts on Facebook, MySpace, or other sites, be sure to list its web address in your profile and in posts. If you use Twitter, include links to your website in what you post.

Search the internet to find places where your website can be listed. Most denominational headquarters' websites provide a place to list all the churches in that denomination, and the listings usually include a web address. People looking for a church may look to the denomination's website to find a church. There are also websites that serve local communities, and they will often list churches in the area. As a rule, we register at any website that appears to be reputable and lists churches. Think about where your target audience hangs out (physically or on the internet), and try to get your web address listed there.

Users can enter keywords on internet search engines such as Google, Bing, and Yahoo!, and the search engines return a ranked list of webpages containing those keywords. (See chapter 8 for instructions about formatting pages to assist search engines.) It is useful but not essential if you register your web address to help search engines find it. I do not recommend paying a company to submit your website to search engine websites. Instead, I recommend registering at Google using this web address: http://google.com/addurl. It is free and can speed traffic to your website when they first index it.

The Ultimate Information Source and Connection for Some

Most people who did not grow up with the internet see it primarily as the ultimate information source—the largest and most automated library in the world. Due to the accessibility, the internet is often their first or main source for information. I am glad that God makes all kinds of people because there is a fanatic of anything and everything, and they create great websites with great information. For example, my mother has purebred bichon frise dogs—cute, white, little fluff balls with a dog inside. Before she got them, I had never heard of the bichon frise breed. I did a web search, and more than two million pages came up on this one breed of dog. I am grateful for all the different kinds of people God created who are now creating websites and contributing to the ultimate information source.

The massive quantities of information on the internet have contributed to the internet culture's need for easy and rapid access to the specific information people desire. The amount of information is overwhelming and growing at an increasing rate. So visitors to your website are typically not going to spend much time systematically reading through everything. Instead, they will move quickly through your website in search of specific information of interest. If they don't find it immediately, they are likely to move on to another website. For this reason, it is important to have a well-organized website that includes search capability. Local search gives visitors the ability to easily find pages by typing in a few keywords. If a visitor finds your website through a search engine or link from another website, then the first page he or she sees may not be the front page. It is important to have complete navigation, including a link to the front page, on every single page. These are all ways to help visitors quickly find the information they seek. Providing excellent content is the best way to keep them coming back.

Those who did not grow up with the internet also like and use information-based interactive features. At our church, we have an online daily devotional, which includes a personal journal to store private notes and a public online community to discuss the devotional topics. Visitors often comment on the current topic and ask or respond to questions. We also have a community prayer exchange page that allows people to post prayer requests. Interactive features encourage visitors to go beyond acquiring information and begin contributing and interacting with others in community. As people interact online, there are additional opportunities to minister to them, and they are more likely to feel a connection to your website and organization.

These visitors also leaped into social networking using online services like Facebook and MySpace. Many people who spend time on the internet often focus on connecting with family and friends through social networking features like their friends list, blog posts, and photo galleries. Social networking simplifies and extends fulfillment of our natural God-given desire to connect in community. Since the church and its community are part of their social network, these websites can be an important way to connect with them.

The Ultimate Cool Place for Others

Young adults and youth who have grown up with the internet accept as common knowledge that it is the ultimate information source. From their perspective, the internet, with its vast sea of information, has always been there. They expect the information to be there, and they are unhappy if it is not.

To them, the internet is less an information source than it is an active place where people go to do everything from hang out to play games to talk with friends. A teenager summarized it well when I asked him why he does not go to our main church website. He said, "There is nothing to do there." That website has lots of information that people seem to appreciate. It even has several interactive features, but from a young person's perspective, "There is nothing to do there." Below are a few things we have observed that help our church connect with people who grew up with the internet.

First, they are essentially online 24/7. If we include text messaging as an internet technology (and it is because even if they are sent and received on a cell phone, the messages travel over that same internet infrastructure), then we can say that most of them are always connected to the internet. From their perspective, the internet is ubiquitous—everywhere. They are web savvy. Computers and the internet way of doing things come naturally. So even if your website navigation and layout are not the best, they will usually be able to find their way around. It is unfortunate that, in many cases, they have few reasons to come to your website. Companies spend millions of dollars on websites designed to attract them and ultimately to generate revenue from the online advertising or sales. The competition for the time they spend on the web is fierce. Although they are on the web frequently, they are probably not on church-related websites, even ones targeted to them.

Second, they want something to do. Instead of simply getting information, they want to post their thoughts, rate something, take a poll, find things, figure out a puzzle, play a game, get rewards or chances to win a prize, create something, or communicate with others. Websites for them should be much more interactive. You don't need to add every possible feature, but you should consider how you can provide opportunities for interactive participation throughout the website.

Third, they are multisensory and multitaskers; they like music and other sound, video, and animation. My twin boys often have multiple instant message boxes on-screen while they are playing a game, listening to music, and watching television—all at the same time. They are more adapted to processing multiple simultaneous stimuli; as a result, they are likely to respond to sound and motion. Since your website is competing with several other things for these people's attention, you are best advised to create pages with less text and focus on the critical message you want to convey. Use links to take visitors to a detail page. I do not think they have a problem focusing on one thing; instead, I think this is merely their way of adapting to the incredible amount of information and stimuli they receive. Once they identify something of interest, they can focus and go deeper. We have many passionate and deep-thinking Christians in our young adult and youth ministries. They just process information in a different way.

Fourth, they often have newer and better computers than the general population, and they are more likely to have high-speed internet access. This is not true everywhere, so you need to assess the people you are serving. For us, knowing our audience has allowed us to add more media and interactivity. For example, we may add a video to the front page of our youth website. This is something we would normally not do on our main church website because people may not be able to play it.

Blind Leading the Blind

When Ginghamsburg Church started its internet ministry, we were surprised that people from other countries visited our website. But we were more surprised to find that people who are visually impaired regularly visit our website. We want to welcome and serve all people, and we had never considered making provisions for people who have special accessibility needs. Worse yet, our internet ministry team learned that we were making browsing more difficult by the way we constructed the website. We really messed up and did not even know we were messing up. One man who attends our church is totally blind. He described for me the special software he uses that reads content and structure from webpages and uses speech synthesis so he can hear what is on those pages. He operates his computer and browses the web all the time with the aid of this software. I am in awe of how God made us able to communicate in different ways. Whether we are typing to talk using instant messaging or we have conditions that reduce our ability to see, we adapt in amazing ways to continue to communicate.

The Web Accessibility Initiative (WAI; www.w3.org/WAI) is designed to help web developers create websites that are more accessible to everyone. Given the church's mission, I think we should lead the way in producing websites that are more accessible to all people. Here are a few tips on how to make websites more accessible (details are available on the w3.org website).

Graphics and Photos

Graphics, including photos, need to include an "alternate" attribute (commonly referred to as "alt-text") that describes a graphic and its purpose. The alt-text is placed in the HTML code for the page to associate a text description with the graphic. If you are using software to create your website, the details of the HTML code are often taken care of automatically, but you still need to remember to enter the alt-text when you add a graphic to a page. The special reader software can read the alt-text out loud to explain what the graphic is. The alt-text will also show up in a regular browser if users move the mouse pointer over a graphic.

Initially, our team did not include alt-text for each of our graphics, and the navigation for our website was done with graphical buttons that contained text in the graphic. The reader software can read text in the webpage but can't read text within an image. As a result, visitors using the special reader software had to guess at the meaning of our navigation buttons. Alt-text would have helped by explaining the function of those graphics. We also used graphics to control the positioning of elements on the page. For example, we had an all-white spacer graphic that created space between columns of text. These graphics, which have no meaning, confused the users of the reader software as they tried to understand the content on the page. The reader had no way of knowing the graphics were only there for spacing. Jesus said, "If one blind person guides another, both will fall into a pit" (Matt. 15:14b). Well, we were blind to these details and clearly were falling "into the pit" and leading others there as well. Now we try to completely avoid using graphics for spacing, and we include alt-text with all graphics and photos.

Video and Audio

All forms of media should include a description that identifies what the audio or video contains. If a transcription of the audio is available, a link to that transcription is helpful.

If your target audience includes people who are hearing impaired, consider obtaining a person to sign American Sign Language (ASL) for worship service videos rather than including only the text transcription. Sign language is often easier for the hearing impaired just as listening to the audio is often easier for a hearing person, and, according to several church members who are deaf and who interpret for the Deaf, many find it easier and more expressive to watch someone sign than to read text transcription. If you have interpreters who translate your worship service to sign language, then you may want to consider recording them and posting the video on your website. Our church tried this for a period of time by providing ASL-interpreted sermons in streaming video each week on our website. The Deaf community appreciated these sermons. Websites for the Deaf even linked to our website and praised our efforts. Unfortunately, we had technical problems with camera positioning and lighting that made the signing difficult to see, so we discontinued it. We learned that the video must be very clear with a high frame rate to help viewers see the motion. However, I continue to believe it is a good idea and encourage you to try it, especially if you have an active ministry for the Deaf.

Hyperlinks

Hyperlinks allow the visitor to change to different pages by clicking a link. It is not uncommon to have many hyperlinks on a page. People who are blind do not have the benefit of seeing the layout of the page and scanning quickly for links. Instead, they need to step through the page or tell the software to generate a list of all the links on the page. The challenge comes from hyperlinks that say things like "Click Here" or just ">>." The context of the page determines the destination of these hyperlinks. The context may be separated from the link due to the way the reader software processes and speaks the words on the page, so it is best to make hyperlinks that are more descriptive.

Make It Accessible

Accessibility is an important consideration for all people we serve. As we are able, we need to help website visitors who may have physical impairments that limit their ability to access a website.

In addition, we need to support visitors with less capable computers and software and slower internet access. For example, most of the international people who are listed at the beginning of this chapter access our website over a telephone line using a modem. We need to be careful not to add features that exclude them. There are people with older computers who simply cannot afford better computers. We need our website to work with less capable computers. For example, it is best to encode audio at a setting like 32K bits/second, which sounds fine and plays over a modem connection as well. For video, offering both a high and a low bandwidth option provides support for both fast and slow connections. We want all visitors to get the best that can be delivered to them.

CHAPTER 5

Designing Your Website

Creating a great-looking website that fits your organization

Every church wants its website to look great, and ours did, too. My first attempt at a design had those shimmering gold buttons that dominated the front page. Most of us agreed that the buttons looked great, even somewhat elegant. But something was wrong. The website just didn't fit us. Ginghamsburg Church is located in the middle of a cornfield (sometimes it is a soybean field or a wheat field), and it is not close to any city. I would never describe us as elegant. We are very informal. People come as they are, and sometimes the pastor preaches while wearing blue jeans. I can't think of anything that is gold in our church, except the connectors on the audio cables. We don't have ornate stained glass windows or a big steeple. Our sanctuary feels more like a living room than the inside of a cathedral. My fancy gold buttons had to go—not because they were bad, but because they didn't fit our DNA.

The second front-page design I provided was quite different and became the first design to go public. The design incorporated a stalk of wheat blowing in the wind with seeds leaving the stalk, and the colors were earth tones. I kept the buttons simple and placed them around the wheat. Designs have changed a lot since late 1996. I can't really say that any of our designs were good by today's standards; however, the design fit us, served us well, and gave people a sense of what our church was like.

Finding Your DNA

What does your organization look and feel like? I am not referring only to the physical building, which is only a small part. I am referring to the personality and the atmosphere. Are you formal or informal? Are you playful or serious? Are you an inner-city church, a suburban church, or a rural church? Are you traditional or contemporary? Are you multicultural? Are you heavily involved in missions? Are you gifted in the arts? Are you small and friendly? I love the diversity of God's creations. Churches are all made of groups of people, yet we are so vastly different. Churches are different in ritual, style, gifts, doctrine, and ministry focus; however, together, we are the body of Christ. Life would be boring if not for all the diversity God created. It is OK to celebrate how God made our churches and us—each with unique DNA.

Having a website design that fits your organization is important because the design is the very first thing visitors see, even before they read anything. The design helps them understand what your organization is about and what it feels like. Translating the characteristics of your organization to a design may seem difficult and abstract. Here is one approach that has helped me: start by browsing many websites. Assess whether they could match your organization. Once you find a few that look like they might fit, combine the best design ideas to create your own design.

What Is in a Design?

The design of a website defines both its overall appearance and the way it operates. Because web design is the subject of full-length books and in-depth design websites, this chapter will focus only on the basics and on the unique aspects of designing websites for Christian organizations. If you'd like more tips on church design, visit Great Church Websites at www.Great ChurchWebsites.org. The creator, David Gillaspey, has many tips on excellent design, and he has personally reviewed thousands of church designs. You can subscribe to see all the churches if you'd like, but the free features alone are valuable. Since design is often a matter of personal preference, please consider the following suggestions as guidelines rather than a strict set of rules.

The design layout defines the location of all elements on the page. Layouts often include a banner graphic across the top that contains the organization's name or logo in the upper left. A footer along the bottom works well for a copyright notice and contact information. On most websites, the main content is partitioned into one to four columns. We started with three columns—narrow columns on the left and right and a wide column in the middle. We liked that look, but over time it became harder to decide which content to place in which column. Then we moved to a two-column layout with the navigation on the left and the main content in a larger right column. For really wide content, such as forums or a calendar, we used a single column. It is OK to select a main column layout and then switch column layouts for different pages as needed to accommodate different types of content, as long as the pages look like they come from the same website. The Web-Empowered Church software now offers the ability to partition a page any way we would like based on our content, which provides maximum layout flexibility.

The design also includes the supporting graphics, colors, and font styles. Supporting graphics can add features such as curves, lines, and shaded regions. They can also include photos and other images. Some organizations like to have a picture of their building on the front page or even part of the design on all pages. That might be OK, especially if the building is distinct; however, the building usually does not tell much about your organization's DNA. The church is the people, not the building. Because churches are all about people, it's probably impossible to have too many pictures of people on a church or other Christian website. As you think about banners at the tops of pages or pictures within the content, make sure there are pictures of people. (See chapter 3 for information on obtaining permission to post a person's photo.)

Most organizations want their website to be inviting and friendly. Lots of pictures of joyful people interacting with one another portray that feeling. Curved lines and gradually shaded regions work well because they seem less harsh. A white or light-colored background with open space around the content feels friendlier. Curved fonts, like Verdana, Arial, and Helvetica, are typically a little easier to read on a screen, especially as the text gets smaller. Textured backgrounds or backgrounds that don't contrast well with the font color can be hard to read and are therefore less inviting. I was asked to review a church website with a bright red background and bright yellow text. I could barely read it. This is not welcoming to visitors. Inviting and friendly websites are pleasant to look at and easy to read.

How Do I Drive This Thing?

Navigation provides the mechanism to move around to different pages on your website. The website should be organized into logical sections and subsections with pages in each. The navigation is usually located along the top or along the left side of each page, but can be on the right. Top navigation frequently lists the main section names evenly spaced in a row. Left-side navigation usually lists pages within a section, in a vertical column similar to a shopping list. Left-side navigation can include the site section and subsection names as well. The advantages of left-side navigation are that it allows the visitor to see the list of links at all times and that the vertical column can accommodate many links.

You can also use dropdown menus that display a list of links when a visitor moves the mouse pointer over a section name at the top of the page. You may not need both a dropdown menu and the left-side navigation. Dropdown menus make sense to most visitors because many computer programs use them, and they can save space on the page by eliminating the need for the left-side navigation. Dropdown menus are a bit more technically challenging to implement across multiple browsers, and they can be more cumbersome for the visitor who must first move the mouse over the section name before seeing a list of pages. The approach you use for navigation is largely a matter of personal preference. Our internet ministry team has tried multiple approaches on our different websites; all have pros and cons, and all work fine.

Another helpful website navigation feature is called "breadcrumbs." Breadcrumbs provide a visual indicator of where the current page is located in the depth of the website. Breadcrumbs usually look something like this: "Home > About Us > Staff" and are positioned near the top navigation. In this example, the current page is the "Staff" page, and it is in the "About Us" section of the website. The words in the breadcrumbs are links to pages at higher levels of the website. In this example, clicking "About Us" would take the visitors up a level to the "About Us" section page, and "Home" would take them back to the front page. Breadcrumbs are not used often by visitors, but they can be handy to visitors who come to the website from a link on another website or from a search engine. The breadcrumbs give visitors a sense of where in the website hierarchy the current page is located. If you are using software that can automatically generate breadcrumbs, or if you have a large website, I suggest that you consider adding breadcrumbs to the design.

I mentioned that navigation is usually positioned along the top or along the left side of a page. Of course, navigation or content can be placed anywhere on a page, but as the web has evolved, most websites have begun to use these general guidelines. By following these guidelines, you help your visitors to learn more quickly the method of navigation for your website.

As much as possible, try to have navigation that is intuitive to your target audience. Navigation is a key method visitors will use to find the content on your website, so it is not the place to be tricky or overly creative. Nothing is more frustrating than a website with difficult navigation. Visitors may give up and leave.

Flash menus are an example of potentially frustrating navigation, so I do not recommend using Flash for navigation. You can use Flash to create beautiful cartoon-like animation with sound. From a technical perspective, Flash works well for creating fancy animated navigation. However, Flash menus behave differently than other approaches, and that can cause confusion. In order to run Flash navigation, the visitor must have the Flash plug-in installed before coming to your website, and Flash will not play on all cell-phone web browsers. Also, the reader software used by the visually impaired is likely to have difficulty interpreting Flash navigation.

Our team needs to do its best to make it easy for visitors to use our website. To learn more about improving usability for your entire website, I recommend a book titled *Don't Make Me Think! A Common Sense Approach to Web Usability*, written by Steve Krug (2nd ed. [Berkeley, Calif.: New Riders, 2006]). This book helped open my eyes to a variety of usability issues. We want visitors to think less about how to operate the website and more about the content, since the content is where the ministry happens.

Just Pick One

You need to choose a design including the appearance and the navigation approach. I suggest that you visit many other websites—internet ministries and others—for a "test drive." Our children's ministry team likes to visit other churches that are doing children's ministry well. They learn by seeing other children's ministries in action. To visit a church, they need to arrange a time when the children's ministry leaders from the other church can meet and travel to the other church. Visiting a church requires a lot of work. One thing that is unique about internet ministry is that you can visit any church internet ministry without ever leaving the comfort of your computer. Take advantage of this opportunity to learn from others. You can also visit commercial websites, which reflect the designs visitors are most used to seeing. Many popular commercial websites pay usability experts to make their websites as intuitive as possible, and they hire expert web designers to create them. We can look at them, learn from them, and implement the best ideas we see. We can't legally use their exact HTML code or graphics from their webpages, but we can learn from and build on their ideas.

It is OK if you don't have team members with web design skills because many web tools come with what are called templates or skins. A website template is a set of files that implement the appearance and navigation of a website. A template can automatically give your website a common look across all its pages. The Web-Empowered Church software comes with several professionally designed templates in different styles and colors. You can change the appearance and navigation of your website at any time by changing the template.

Once you pick a design, you should use it consistently across the entire website. When our team first started our church's site, we tried to create a different design for each major section. We quickly found that each section felt like an entirely new website, and that was confusing for visitors. Of course, the design does not need to be exactly the same on every page. You can vary graphical elements or colors for different sections. That helps visitors identify the sections, and they will not be confused as long as the pages look consistent and operate in a similar way. In addition, if you include other websites such as social networking, external calendars, or external online stores in your web ministry, do your best to make those systems match the overall appearance of your main website. For some external websites like Facebook, you have few options to customize the appearance, but you can at least use a common profile image that identifies your organization. Visitors will probably know they are going to different websites, but it helps the websites feel like they are part of one ministry.

Don't agonize over finding the "perfect" design. There is no perfect design, and there is no design that everyone will love. The time may come when you simply must choose. Just pick a design and know that you can change it as time goes on. Even the best design will need to be changed later for variety and to evolve with changing design trends. Remember, the content remains the most important part of the website. Visitors come back because of the content.

CHAPTER 6

Understanding the Technologies

Learning to use the basic technologies needed for web ministry

First, there were acronyms: HTML, XHTML, CSS, XML, RSS, SQL, PHP, and CMS, just to name a few. Then there were "bumpy" words like JavaScript, then hyphenated words like e-mail and e-store, and then made-up words like podcast and webinar.

It is difficult to learn something by reading if you can't understand the words you are reading. My internet ministry team was also surprised to learn that even the people who were using these words were not always sure what they stood for, but we needed to learn the language of the internet ministry tools we were using. Otherwise, we would not be able to understand statements like "Podcasting is really just RSS with an added enclosure tag," or "Our CMS is written in PHP with a MySQL database." At first, it seemed impossible to get it all straight, but as we learned the lingo, we found that we began to "talk funny," too.

This chapter and the next two chapters are meant to be safe, guided tours of the terms and the tools in your internet ministry technology toolbox. This chapter discusses the fundamental tools that make your website go. Chapter 7 introduces you to multimedia power tools used for graphics, animation, audio, and video. Chapter 9 explains free web services like Facebook and Twitter. For each technology tool, you will learn what it is, what it is good for, and suggested tool choices. This is not a survey of all tools—that would clutter both your mind and mine. Instead, I will try to focus on the tools you need to know and the essential information you need to know about them. You will also learn what the common buzzwords and acronyms mean. In my experience, most technology is not as scary when you get past the hype and the terminology and understand what it does. You won't learn exactly how to implement each tool because that depth of information would not fit in this book; however, since these are the tools used by most internet developers, there are many books and online resources that can provide more details. Please fasten your seat belt and enjoy this guided tour.

Web Browsers and Web Servers

Computers and computer networks existed prior to the development of what we know as the internet. Web browser and web server software made the internet possible and usable. A man named Tim Berners-Lee built the first web browser and web server in 1990. So the very first internet ministry tool was created in 1990. After that, the internet grew slowly; the first church websites were not created until the mid- to late 1990s. Most kinds of ministries in your church have been around for hundreds or even a couple thousand years, but internet ministry is just a baby.

A web browser is the software installed on your computer that allows you to access websites on the internet. Internet Explorer, Firefox, Safari, and Google Chrome are just a few common browsers. When you type a web address into your web browser or when you click a link on a webpage, the web browser communicates over the internet with the specific web server defined in the web address. The web address also designates a requested file and can pass some additional data. Web servers are computers on the internet running web server software. Web servers wait for requests from browsers. When a request comes in, the web server either gets the file from its hard drive or generates the file dynamically, and in the process the web server may also store some information. The web server then sends the file to the browser. A web browser may send multiple requests in order to get all the files associated with a webpage. For example, if there is a graphic on a webpage, the browser will process the page file and then see that a graphic file is needed. The web browser will then send out another request to the web server asking for the additional graphic file. Each one of these requests that a web browser sends to a web server is referred to as a "hit." You may hear website statistics that refer to "hits per day" or "hits per month."

A browser maintains a cache (pronounced "cash"). *Cache* is one of those technology words you will hear at different times. Caching is the storing of retrieved information that might be reused later; caching speeds the retrieval process. By storing the first copy of a retrieved file, the browser can just grab the locally stored copy in the future instead of sending another request over the internet. For example, let's say you have a common banner graphic on every page of your website. When a new user comes to the site, the browser will request the banner graphic file from the server; however, for future pages, the browser can just grab the banner graphic file from your local computer because the file is automatically stored in the browser cache.

As the browser receives the files or retrieves them from the local cache, it builds the view of a webpage from the contents of those files. The view is what you see as the webpage. A web browser's main function is to get files from web servers and to render (create the display of) pages. A web server's main function is to send requested files to browsers.

No one can control which browsers visitors use to view a website. This is one technology website designers can't pick. One of the challenges of building webpages is creating them in a way that they can be rendered correctly by many different types of browsers. The next sections include tips on browser compatibility, but this issue remains a challenge for all website developers.

HTML and the Other Family Members

HTML stands for "HyperText Markup Language." HTML is the main language of the internet—it is what is used to create webpages. Don't worry about memorizing what HTML stands for; most people just call it HTML. The latest version of HTML is more accurately called XHTML, which stands for "eXtensible HTML." XHTML is the recommended modern-day language to create webpages. XHTML is a little more strict and specific than the old HTML; therefore, different types of browsers render it more consistently. You will hear HTML and XHTML used interchangeably in normal web conversation, but just know that the XHTML specification is the one to use. The main specifications for most web languages are located on the World Wide Web Consortium (W3C) at www.w3.org.

When a browser requests a webpage, the file that is returned contains HTML. If you look at the file, the file just contains characters. These characters tell the web browser how to render the page. The instructions for the web browsers are referred to as "tags." Tags are enclosed in less-than and greater-than signs. Here are some examples of common tags: <body>, <p>, <h1>, and <div>. Most tags have a start and an end tag. The end tag is indicated by a preceding forward slash, for example: </body>, </p>, </h1>, and </div>. A few tags do not have a separate end tag, so the slash is added to the end of the start tag, for example: <br/>. If you view a webpage file in a simple text editor, you will see text from the webpage intermingled with various tags that instruct the browser. There are many different tags with different sorts of instructions. How much you need to learn about HTML depends on how involved you are with the underlying construction of webpages, but it remains beneficial to know about HTML tags and how they are used. The good news is that modern-day web editors write the HTML for you most of the time, so you don't need to rush to learn all the details.

Lots of different browser-like programs are going to read your webpage HTML, including multiple types of web browsers, special reader software for the visually impaired, and search engine programs. To maximize the likelihood that all these different programs will understand your webpages correctly, try to use valid XHTML on your website. The W3C has an online tool that can check your pages for you. You can automatically check a page for valid XHTML by using their markup validation service at validator.w3.org. Most browsers will render a page, even with minor errors; however, the best and safest approach is to use correct XHTML.

XHTML is really part of the eXtensible Markup Language (XML) family of languages. XML is becoming increasingly popular, especially for storing or exchanging data. In XHTML, the tags are provided, but in XML you can define your own tags. The tags use the same format with less-than and greater-than signs. XML can tag any kind of data, and if a program writes information to an XML-formatted file, then another program that knows what the custom tags mean can read the information.

RSS and Podcasting

RSS stands for "Rich Site Summary" or "Really Simple Syndication." Like a lot of other web terms, many people who use the term "RSS" probably don't know what it stands for. RSS is also in the XML family of markup languages, so it has the familiarly formatted tags, but it also has a specific set of tags used to define an index of items on a website. The purpose of RSS is to provide an up-to-date summary of available information on a website. That information is read by RSS reader software. Visitors can use websites that include online RSS readers like Google Reader or RSS reader programs on a local computer like NewzCrawler and NetNewsWire (which works on the Apple iPad and iPhone as well). RSS readers are ideally suited for smart phones because they provide summarized information that fits well on the phone's smaller screen, and they can conserve bandwidth and memory.

The RSS readers retrieve designated RSS formatted files from one or more websites. The RSS reader uses the RSS files to provide the visitor with a quick summary of updated items on a website without requiring the visitor to browse the website. If the visitor wants more information, then he or she can click a link, and the web browser will go to the page on the website where the information is located. Initially, RSS was used largely for news feeds. Visitors can get a quick summary of the latest news stories and click any that are of interest. Churches can use RSS for items like blogs, news, events, Bible studies, and sermons. Any popular list of items that changes over time can be included in what is called an "RSS feed." Tell visitors about the RSS feeds you offer by listing links to the RSS files on your website. Visitors need those links to tell the RSS reader software which RSS feeds to access.

RSS is a mechanism to help people manage and find the information they are looking for without browsing websites or sorting through large amounts of extraneous information. As we all experience information overload from the incredible quantity of information on the internet, mechanisms like RSS and the associated RSS reader programs become more popular. They are a nice feature for an organization's website.

To create an RSS feed, you need to create the special index file on your website and then keep it up to date. Creating the file manually can be challenging and is prone to error. The best approach is to include software on your website that will automatically generate RSS files based upon updates to your website. Content management systems can do this automatically for certain types of lists.

Podcasting is a derivative of RSS and is used to distribute the latest versions of audio or video files. A podcast reader reads an index of the available audio or video files. Unlike RSS, the audio or video files are often automatically downloaded. If the visitor has an iPod or other portable media player, the files can be automatically downloaded to that player. The term "podcast" comes from combining the word *iPod* and the word *broadcast*. But a podcast does not send out a continuous signal like a broadcast does. Instead, the receiving computer actively requests the audio or video files from the server. From the web server's point of view, podcast files are not really special. They are simply audio or video files sent out in response to a web browser request, so you don't need any special web server software to podcast.

Podcasts work well for sermons or other periodic teachings. Since podcasts can be automatically downloaded, they are one way to make content more available and accessible. We have created audio podcasts of our pastor's sermons and a weekly Bible study for some time. People who use them tell us they like the podcast because it makes the content portable. For example, they can listen to a sermon while exercising, driving, or traveling for business. For a church, sermon audio or video podcasts are probably not going to be more popular than sermon audio or video displayed on webpages. However, if the sermons already exist on the website in the correct audio or video format, then all you need to do to make those files available via a podcast is to create and maintain the podcast file itself and to tell people about it. After that, the podcast reader programs do all the work.

The podcast file is nearly identical to an RSS file except for an additional tag called an "enclosure tag." The enclosure tag provides information about the audio or video file, including its location, size, and type. Since the files may be quite large, the included file size lets the program know the size before it downloads the file. As with RSS, you will benefit from automating the generation of the podcast file; it can be error prone and difficult to keep up to date.

CSS

As I mentioned earlier, CSS stands for "Cascading Style Sheets." CSS styles tell a web browser how to visually display HTML elements on your website. Prior to CSS, the format of the content was defined by format tags embedded in the HTML. This made maintenance very difficult. For example, if you wanted all your paragraph titles to be centered instead of justified, you would need to go into each page in the website and make this change. This proved to be an inefficient approach because the formatting tags were repeated over and over in the pages. Those old format tags can still be used, but I do not recommend that. With CSS, a paragraph title tagged with an <H2> tag can be changed across the website by setting the CSS style for the H2 tag in a common CSS file. In just one place, CSS tells the browser how to format the HTML elements throughout the website. CSS styles define many features like location, alignment, background color, foreground color, spacing, borders, size, and fonts.

On our church's website, we transitioned from the old embedded HTML format tags to the new world of CSS and use the TYPO3 Content Management System (CMS). It took some time, but the new pages are much easier to maintain, and they look better. In our case, we could not avoid this situation—CSS did not exist when we first built our website. The nature of technology is that it evolves. We must evolve with technology to get its benefits. We do not often enjoy change—we attempt to manage it—but the fact that change happens should not be a surprise; it is just the nature of technology.

Unlike XHTML and RSS, CSS is not in the XML family of markup languages. (That was a lot of acronyms! If you mostly understood that sentence, you are learning techie talk.) CSS does not use XML tag formatting. Instead, a CSS file includes a list of the HTML elements with the settings for various attributes of the elements enclosed in curly braces, "{"and"}." (Note that quotation marks in HTML need to be "straight quotes," meaning they do not curve around the word or words between them.) The word *cascading* in "Cascading Style Sheets" refers to the fact that styles defined first remain in effect within the page unless they are overridden with later style definitions. Also, styles applied to HTML elements are applied to HTML elements inside them. For example, the HTML body tag (<body> and </body>) must surround all the page content. If a style for the body tag includes a font attribute using this style rule "body {font-family: times}" then the font "times" will be applied to all text on the page unless it is overridden by a style rule after the body tag. The styles cascade down through the HTML on the page.

Styles can be stored in a separate file or within the HTML. If you store the main styles for your website in a file, browsers can cache the file and reuse it to render other pages. A separate file eases maintenance because a change to one style will affect that style for all the pages on your website. Tools like the TYPO3 CMS can generate the CSS file automatically.

JavaScript

JavaScript is a scripting language embedded into the HTML to add interactivity to the webpage. There are other scripting languages, but JavaScript is the most popular and universal. JavaScript is not the programming language called Java. Although the two programming languages have some similarities, they have totally different functionalities. The initial purpose of JavaScript was to add webpage functions such as dynamically changing HTML, responding to events like a mouse click, validating data entered into a web form, detecting the browser type, and creating or reading browser cookies. In recent years, developers have pushed JavaScript to its limit by writing advanced applications in JavaScript such as rich text editors that provide word processing features inside a browser. The trend is certainly moving toward adding more JavaScript to improve usability, adding more moving visual effects, and adding more advanced interactive behavior to websites. This interactive functionality is a feature of "Web 2.0," which refers to the second generation of web interfaces and capabilities.

"Cookie" is an unusual name for a mechanism that allows a webpage to write data to a small file on the visitor's computer. When the visitor returns to the website, the browser automatically sends the data in the cookie file to the web server. JavaScript or server software will react based on the data in the cookie. Cookies are commonly used to remember preferences or to automatically log on to a website. On our church's website, if a visitor logs on with a username and password, and does not log out, we use cookies to automatically log the visitor back on during his or her next visit. In the past, there were privacy and security concerns associated with cookies. Although those concerns have been addressed, some people still disable cookies in their browser settings. So on pages we create, we cannot always count on cookies to be an available option because some people have disabled them.

JavaScript is either embedded into an HTML page or placed in a separate file. The HTML "script" tag is used to tell the browser to interpret a section of the file as JavaScript instead of HTML. That tag looks like "<script type="text/javascript">" or just "<script>." The closing tag is "</script>."

JavaScript is a programming language, so it can be difficult to learn and understand. If you have the need to learn JavaScript, there are many examples of JavaScript on the internet, and these examples perform most common functions. There are lots of online resources that can teach you JavaScript, and libraries of prewritten JavaScript are available to simplify JavaScript development. In most cases, it is not necessary to learn how to program in JavaScript, but it is an important part of web development since some page functions require it.

Server-Side Scripting

Server-side scripting is similar to JavaScript except that the script runs on the web server instead of within the browser. Server-side scripting is the programming used to dynamically generate pages for your website. For example, you may want to include a different Bible verse each day on the front page of your website. You would not want to store the Bible verse as part of a permanent webpage because you would need to manually change it every day. However, server-side scripting can read a verse from a file containing different verses and automatically change the verse for the day as part of generating the webpage. This is a very simple example. Server-side scripting can do many powerful functions, and the scripts can be quite large, even many thousands of lines long. These scripts do all the processing needed to create your dynamic and interactive website.

There are many server-side scripting languages. The two most popular are Microsoft's Active Server Pages (ASP), which is more accurately referred to as "ASP.NET," and Personal Home Page (PHP), which is an open-source solution. These two server-side scripting systems are both popular and full featured. Either one is a good choice.

ASP.NET is commercial software from Microsoft. It is a good choice if your organization is a heavy user of advanced Microsoft software or if there are people on your team who already know ASP.NET. As commercial software, ASP.NET has the advantage of additional documentation, training, and technical support. You will need to set up a Microsoft Windows server to run ASP.NET, so you will probably pay more than you would with open-source software because the Windows Server software is fairly expensive. Also, in my experience, ASP.NET may require more web server memory and processing power. ASP.NET is popular for use on large corporate websites.

Unlike ASP.NET, PHP is licensed as open-source software, and that license gives you the right to use the software and modify it without paying for it. The original authors retain copyright ownership of the software, so you cannot sell it or remove copyright notices from it. Besides being free, another advantage of open-source software is that anyone can get the software source code files used to create the program. Most people simply use the software and don't work with the source code, but having the source code allows you the option of modifying or enhancing the software. If you modify the software, then you can use it freely and can also submit the modifications to the open-source project for possible incorporation into a future official release of the software. In this way, the community of users can contribute to making the software better. Open-source software is often developed by people with varied skills and motivations who contribute to the project without being directly paid for their work, so the quality may vary substantially. In general, the quality and documentation for commercial software are more consistent than those of open-source software. PHP is a large and popular open-source project, so the quality and documentation for PHP are excellent. And, it is free, too!

Open-source software matches the way many Christian organizations think and operate. Most churches are concerned about keeping costs down, and open-source software provides significant capabilities at no cost. Moreover, churches encourage people with different skills and gifts to join in community to work together and volunteer time, which is how open-source software is created and maintained. Church communities often give freely and substantially for the common good and the benefit of others. And, of course, open-source software is free. I am not saying that there is any sort of divine connection to open source, but I do think that open source makes sense to Christians and that we should seriously consider this option for acquiring software within Christian organizations.

Because it is open source, PHP is developed by a community of actual users focused on an excellent server-side scripting system for creating webpages. The result is that PHP is popular, full featured, and tailored for web development. One measure of PHP's popularity is the website HotScripts.com, which provides scripts you can use on your website. HotScripts currently lists over five times as many PHP scripts as scripts in the next-largest server-side scripting language. While it is unlikely you will use most of these scripts, they are an indicator of the popularity of PHP.

Both ASP.NET and PHP are good choices; however, I recommend PHP due to its capabilities, popularity, and reduced web server software costs. Also, PHP is the scripting language used to write the TYPO3 software. Thanks to tools like TYPO3, you will probably need to know very little server-side scripting. If you need to learn PHP, there are many books available, and php.net is a good reference.

Databases

Databases store and retrieve information on a website. Server-side scripting generates the pages, but databases manage the website data. For example, a database can store a list of events in a calendar. Each event could include a date, title, and description. By using the event data in the database, server-side scripting can generate a page that lists the next ten events or a page that displays the current month's calendar. Website visitors see up-to-date information because these pages change automatically as events change and as time passes. As websites become increasingly automated and interactive, the need for databases increases. In fact, since databases add such flexibility, the trend is to store most website content in a database. This has been common for commercial websites for years.

Databases require separate database software running on your web server or a companion server. Microsoft SQL Server is an example of a commercial database program. MySQL is a popular example of an open-source database program. There are other database programs as well. A database program is installed and available as part of a typical web server computer. The acronym "SQL," which is used in database program names, stands for "Structured Query Language." Most people refer to it by the letters "S-Q-L" and pronounce it like the word *sequel*. SQL is the common language programmers use to command the database software to perform functions such as storing and retrieving data. Server-side scripting sends a command called a "query" to the database server. The database software stores data in a combination of special internal files and computer memory, and returns data to the server-side scripting in response to a query. For example, when a user is constructing a calendar, a SQL query could request all calendar events for the current month. This information would then be returned to the server-side scripting for use on a webpage.

A database is a group of data defined by a database name and protected with a username and password. Database software may store many different databases. A database is divided into tables, each with a unique table name. A table is a list of similar data, such as a calendar-events table or a registered website visitor table. Each table is made up of individual records. A record is one element in a table, such as one calendar-event record or one registered website visitor record. Records are made up of multiple fields. Database software supports different types of fields for storing different types of data such as date, number, and text fields.

For example, a database might have a table named "Events," which contains one record for each stored event. Each event record might have three fields: event date, event title, and event description. This simple database table structure can support a church-event system that could store, retrieve, and display many church events.

Content Management System (CMS)

A content management system (CMS) is a combination of server-side scripting, data files, and a database. These are all installed and run on a web server connected to the internet. A CMS is usually large in terms of the amount of server resources it requires including the total number of files, needed disk space, required memory, and required processing power. Commercial CMS packages can be very expensive. Traditionally, only large companies have been able to afford a CMS, but changes in technology and the arrival of open-source versions like TYPO3, Joomla, and Drupal have helped make CMS software more commonly available.

As the name indicates, a CMS is a system used to manage the content for websites. A CMS stores content in files and database tables and then uses the stored information to dynamically generate webpages. A CMS allows you to create and maintain a website and to add interactive features. TYPO3 and some other CMS packages have special administrative webpages that allow you to create a website using a standard web browser on your personal computer. With a proper username and password, you can make updates to your website from any computer connected to the internet. In fact, multiple people can help maintain your website, even at the same time.

Besides being a handy way to develop and maintain a website, a CMS has some other useful features. With a CMS, the look and feel of the website are separated from the content. "Look" and "feel" refer to the overall appearance of your website (look) and the way the website operates, including navigation (feel). The CMS accomplishes this separation by using templates (sometimes called skins). As I mentioned in chapter 5, templates are a series of files, including CSS, and settings that define the website look and feel. Templates define characteristics such as layout, banners, curves, lines, buttons, navigation, menus, sidebars, breadcrumbs, headers, footers, colors, and fonts. One powerful feature of templates is that they take care of formatting automatically so that you can enter content without manually adding the website-wide formatting. Before we started using TYPO3, we had to manually set fonts and other formatting as we entered the content. That made both content entry and maintenance more challenging. Templates allow you to change the entire look and feel of your website in seconds, giving it a fresh look while preserving all the content.

Another unique feature of a CMS, and TYPO3 in particular, is database-driven dynamic content display. For any page or for the content on any page, you can set a start date for it to appear and an end date for it to disappear. The content is then displayed only during the specified range of dates. We often use this feature to keep the website automatically up-to-date. During one summer we had many camps, so we created a page that listed and described each of the camps and provided links on that page for all the camps. By appropriately setting the correct end dates for every camp, we managed the information automatically. Each camp page disappeared the day after the camp was over. The day after the last camp ended, the entire page disappeared from our website. This was all automatic once we set the dates. Some churches switch to a CMS for this feature alone. The content elements that automatically disappear from a website are not deleted; they are simply hidden from the public. You can reuse them by updating the content and adjusting the dates.

In addition to setting start and end dates, you can use dynamic content display to limit access to a page (or specific content within a page) to a particular set of visitors. Visitors log on by using their usernames and passwords, and they see different content based on what they are authorized to access. We use this feature for sections of the website limited to church staff, certain leaders, or various other groups. This powerful tool enables volunteers to access from anywhere special information that helps them serve the church. For example, our music team can privately post the schedule for weekends and events, along with the planned song titles, but only the music team members can access this information.

I strongly encourage you to use a CMS to assist in creating your internet ministry. The alternative is to create individual pages that are posted on your website. The non-CMS approach could work for small websites, but as your web ministry grows, as you want more people to help update the website, and as your website becomes more community-based and interactive, a CMS will quickly become essential. There are so many choices for CMS software that the choices become confusing. From our team's experience, I recommend TYPO3 CMS. The Web-Empowered Church Starter Package includes TYPO3 preconfigured with features for Christian organizations. Today, most any significant commercial website uses a CMS. Churches should have those same benefits.

CHAPTER 7

Making Media

Deploying graphics, animation, audio, and video

When I set out to build our church's first webpage, I decided to add a custom graphic. Adding a graphic to a page seemed pretty straightforward. I created a simple graphic. That wasn't too difficult; in fact, it was even fun. However, when I tried to save the graphic, the program I was using offered me a choice of thirty-one different file formats in which to save, including many options I had never seen before. I had a one in thirty-one (or 3.2 percent) chance of guessing the right one. Options are supposed to be good, but they don't feel good when you don't have any clue which one to pick.

As we continued on the journey to build Ginghamsburg.org, it seemed like each technical feature we added to the site resulted in another time-consuming investigation to figure out what technologies were available, what they could do, which one we should use, and how to use it. We think of these investigations as adventures because each one seemed to be a somewhat painful exploration filled with unexpected twists, turns, and dead ends.

Once I figured out the right graphics file format to use and got some pages working, we decided to add videos of our weekly sermons. Oh, no—another adventure! We learned that some video formats must be downloaded before they will play. Other formats can download and play at the same time. Some won't play on some computers. Some require an uncommon browser plug-in. Some require special server software that we could not afford. And none of them did everything right. There are many cool technologies to use on your website, but the adventure of understanding them and deciding which ones to use can be unpleasant.

This chapter continues a guided tour of web technologies with an overview of media tools. This is not a survey of all tools, but an introduction to the tools you need to know and the essential information you need to know about them.

Graphics

Photographs, cartoons, and other images add to the appearance and communication of a website. Some of the main web graphic file formats are Graphics Interchange Format (GIF), Joint Photographic Experts Group (JPG or JPEG), and Portable Network Graphics (PNG). Each can display any graphic, but the file size and the quality of the resulting image may vary substantially. It is best to save graphics in the default file format that your graphics program (Photoshop, InDesign, and so on) uses. These source files will probably be much larger than JPGs, GIFs, or PNGs, and they will not display on the web. But using the default format makes it easier to modify the graphic in the future and ensures the graphics retain their maximum quality. When you are ready to put a graphic on your website, you can save it to a web-compatible format if it is not already saved in that format.

GIF: A GIF-formatted graphic can contain 256, 16, or 2 distinct colors in its color palette. A graphic is made up of a series of dots often referred to as "pixels," and the color palette contains the list of all colors used in the graphic. Each pixel is set to one color in the color palette. In order to reduce the file size required to store the color palette and the many pixel colors, GIF files are compressed. The GIF compression method is lossless, which means that the final image displayed is not altered by the compression process. For very simple images made up of just a few colors, reducing the color palette to 16 colors can substantially shrink the file size. Due to the limited color palette, GIFs work best for cartoon-like graphics that use few colors or when large regions of the graphic contain one solid color. Logos and buttons usually work well in GIF format. These types of graphics should display with good quality, and the file size should be lower.

GIF also supports setting one of the colors in the color palette to transparent, which means that any pixels set to the transparent color will not be filled. The transparent pixels will display whatever colors are behind the graphic. For example, if the background color of your website is white, the transparent pixels will display the color white, but if the background color changes to black, then those same transparent pixels will display the color black.

One of the fun aspects of GIF graphics is that you can animate them, which is a feature not found in JPG and PNG graphics. To animate a GIF, you create a sequence of individual GIF graphics and combine them into one file with your graphics program (for example, Photoshop). Each graphic is a frame in the animation sequence. The animation sequence is controlled by setting the time delay between frames and setting whether the sequence loops through the frames forever or stops at the last frame. The final animated GIF file size is the total of the size of each of the frames in the sequence. The files can get large very quickly, so it is important to minimize the number of frames.

The thing to remember with GIF-formatted graphics is that the color palette is small; when you save a graphic to GIF format, the graphics program will select colors to fill the palette. If you have too many colors in your image, the program will change them and may use a technique called "dithering." With dithering, pixels that are side by side are set to colors in the palette that produce the desired color if the two colors are combined. For example, a light blue region of color might be filled with alternating dark blue and white pixels. The result is something close to the original image, but it may look a bit grainy or textured. Dithering is a common technique and can be seen by looking very closely at your television screen. From a distance, it looks clear, but up close it looks like a mess of different colors.

Currently, everyone can freely use GIF graphic files. Previously, Unisys owned patents on the GIF format. However, it appears that the last GIF software patent expired by 2004.

PNG: Previously, in response to concern that Unisys might force everyone to start paying to use the GIF format, a new graphics format called PNG was created. PNG is an open standard. You can use PNG graphics in place of GIF graphics, but there are a few differences. The PNG format supports millions of colors, while the GIF format supports only up to 256. Like GIF compression, PNG compression is lossless, but PNG compression has the added advantage that it usually produces smaller files than GIF compression. PNG graphics support transparency, but some older browsers do not properly display PNG transparency. PNG graphics do not support animation, but nonetheless, PNG files are increasingly popular.

JPG: The JPG format supports millions of colors—16,777,216 colors to be exact—and high levels of compression. Unlike GIF and PNG compression, JPG compression can be adjusted. Raising the compression factor reduces both the quality of the graphic and the file size. JPG graphics also include an option called "progressive encoding," which allows a graphic to display before it is completely downloaded. Initially the image is somewhat unclear, but the detail fills in as the remainder of the graphic is downloaded. JPG graphics do not support transparency or animation.

The JPG format is perfect for photographs. Photographs are substantially smaller in JPG format than in GIF or PNG. The quality of the photographic image usually looks better than it does in GIF format because the JPG format supports so many colors. We commonly set the JPG compression factor to about 10 percent, and the difference between the original graphic and the final JPG is nearly undetectable if you look at the two images side by side.

If you are unsure about compression settings or whether or not to use JPG, GIF, or PNG, use your graphics program to save the file to multiple formats and then compare file sizes and appearance. The quality of the image and the resulting file size vary substantially due to the content of the graphic. Sometimes you need to experiment and then pick the best one. Of course, the smaller the files are, the faster they will download for a website visitor.

Browser Plug-ins

Plug-ins are separate software that visitors download and install to add features to a browser. For example, a plug-in can enable a video to play in a webpage or a formatted document to display inside the browser. The challenge with relying on plug-ins is that visitors may not have them installed, may not feel comfortable installing them, or may not be able to install them. Unless a plug-in provides an important feature, it is best to require only common plug-ins that are most likely to be installed and ready to run on your visitors' computers. Below are a few common plug-ins and recommendations about their use.

Java Applets: Java applets are small programs that can run inside a browser. The issue with Java is that some visitors may have Java disabled because of rumors of security issues. Also, Java is quite large to download and somewhat sluggish when it runs. Part of the sluggishness is caused by the fact that Java applets can be large and can take time to initialize and run. So, in most cases, it is probably best to stay away from Java.

ActiveX: ActiveX is similar to Java. As with Java, you can develop powerful applications that run as ActiveX controls. However, based on browser security settings, ActiveX may be disabled, or a visitor may need to click a warning message before the ActiveX control can download. The biggest issue with ActiveX is that it is a Microsoft technology that will not work in some browsers or may work only after installing special plug-ins. For these reasons, it is probably better to avoid using ActiveX.

Flash: Flash was developed by Macromedia, which is a company that was purchased by Adobe Systems. Flash is a powerful and versatile multimedia technology that supports animation, interactivity, audio, and video. Flash applications are often referred to as "Flash movies." Flash movies are surprisingly small considering the amount of media they contain. Since Flash is very popular, it is one of the most commonly installed and used plug-ins. Using Flash movies is fairly straightforward, but creating Flash movies is hard. The challenges with creating a custom Flash include the cost of purchasing commercial Flash development software and the technical challenge of learning and developing Flash. Custom Flash development is a special skill among web developers. Fortunately, you do not need to own the development software or be a Flash developer to use existing Flash movies on a website.

On ministry websites, Flash has many possibilities. For example, Flash works well for interactive games and animated teaching or storytelling. We have used Flash for multimedia e-cards—web-based greeting cards that visitors can select, personalize, and send to others by email. The resulting e-cards, which are displayed in a webpage, include animation and music. The e-cards can be quite beautiful and emotionally moving.

Some organizations like Flash so well that they choose to do entire websites with Flash. I strongly discourage you from doing this because it can be very difficult to maintain. In addition, the navigation and behavior of the website are often not intuitive to visitors who are used to navigating non-Flash-based websites.

HTML5

The HTML standard is evolving to include more interactivity, animation, and media functions without the need for Flash or other browser plug-ins. Standard HTML now includes features like drop-down menus that visually slide down and up, interactive photo slide shows with animated transitions between images, dragging and dropping elements on a page, and displaying a larger version of an image overlaid on top of a page. These features are implemented with HTML, CSS, and Javascript, and require web browsers that support them. HTML version 5 (HTML5) adds many interactive media features that were previously not possible in HTML, such as playing audio and video without a browser plug-in.

As HTML evolves, web developers create powerful tools written in Javascript and HTML that enable you to easily add interactive features to your website. For example, SmoothGallery is a common script that we use regularly for easy-to-use and visually appealing photo slideshows or rotating banners. As these tools become available and HTML evolves, it is better to use HTML features instead of browser plug-ins as long as you are confident that your website visitors have the needed browser version. An added advantage of HTML solutions is that text within them can be read and indexed by search engines.

PDF

PDF stands for "Portable Document Format." PDF is a popular file format for creating electronic versions of paper documents. You can use PDF-generation software to print a complex document to a PDF file (instead of a printer), and the resulting electronic document file will look almost exactly like the paper document. The PDF file retains all the original document fonts, graphics, and formatting. If you upload PDF files to your website, visitors have the option of downloading the PDF file and printing it. The free Adobe Reader plug-in is required to view and print the PDF document, but this plug-in is very common, so most people should have access to it.

PDF files are ideal when you want to post a highly formatted document to a website so people can download and print the document file. PDF files work well for forms that require signatures, like our student-ministry permission forms that require parents' signatures.

Many churches use PDF files way too often because PDF files are easy to create from existing files that are intended to be paper documents. If you have a document stored on your computer and you print it to a PDF file, then you quickly have something to post on your website. Unfortunately, PDF files are not well suited for online reading because most people prefer not to read PDF files on a computer screen. PDF files can be slow to download, and the PDF plug-in works differently from most website navigation. When visitors click a link to a PDF, they may feel like they've left the website.

If your visitors need to read information online, it is usually best to post the content on standard webpages. Having said that, there may be times when you should post content in PDF. Some paper documents are long and have a great deal of formatting. For example, our "Events and Classes" brochure is quite long and packed with specially formatted information. We choose to post it in PDF because it would take an incredible amount of time to extract the information from the brochure to post it online, and people tend to read the paper version anyway. So the electronic copy in PDF is an easy way to provide a backup copy for anyone who needs it. The same is true with our weekly bulletin. It is highly formatted, and everyone in church already gets a paper copy, but we post it in PDF as well in case someone wishes to reference it online.

A printable webpage is an alternative to a PDF and can work exceptionally well in most cases. A printable webpage is specially styled with a template designed to support printing to paper instead of viewing online. Typically, banners and other webpage-specific formatting are removed or minimized to make the page look cleaner and to prepare it for printing. A printable page is still a standard webpage. We use this technique for most of our content that is likely to be printed, such as text sermons and Bible studies. We like this approach because (1) with the help of the content management system, the same content can be automatically used to display both online pages and printable pages; (2) with modern cascading style sheet styling, the printed document can be close to the quality of a PDF document when it is printed; (3) the printable webpage is more easily read online, and some people prefer to read that version; and (4) printing a printable webpage does not require any plug-in; the visitor merely prints the page from the browser.

Audio

In the past, there have been many competing audio file formats to use for web audio; however, the MP3 file format is now most popular. MP3 stands for "MPEG Audio Layer-3." Compared to other audio formats, such as WAV (Waveform audio format), MP3 file sizes tend to be smaller for the same audio quality. This, plus the popularity of portable MP3 players, has contributed to widespread use of the MP3.

One challenge with placing audio files on your website is that the files tend to be larger than other web files. If you store a lot of audio files, running out of disk space on your server may become an issue. However, the bigger issue is usually the time it takes visitors who are connected to the internet via a telephone line and a modem to download these files. A thirty-minute sermon typically results in a 7.2 megabyte MP3 file, which takes about thirty minutes to download for a dial-up visitor. Waiting thirty minutes would disappoint visitors who want to listen immediately to the sermon.

Progressive download is a technique that allows an audio or video file to play while it is downloading, normally from a web server. A browser plug-in downloads a portion of the beginning of the file first and stores it in the computer's memory. This is called "buffering." Then the file starts playing from the beginning. The file plays as the download process continues simultaneously. As long as the downloaded portion of the file stays ahead of the portion of the file that is playing, the file will continue to play to the end without pausing. With a dial-up modem connection, a visitor can listen to an entire thirty-minute sermon after waiting about twenty seconds to begin. If the download cannot keep up, the player will pause for a few seconds to allow more of the file to download into the buffer, and then it will continue playing. Progressive download works well for fast connections, too, because the audio begins playing almost immediately.

For MP3, I recommend three mechanisms for delivery. First, use a free Flash MP3 player (available from Web-Empowered Church) that supports progressive download. Since it is Flash, no additional plug-in is required. With progressive download, visitors will hear an MP3 file start to play shortly after they click the play button. Second, provide a link to the MP3 file so the visitor can download it to play later or to manually copy to a portable MP3 player. Clicking the link can also cause the MP3 to play inside whatever MP3 player program a visitor has on his or her computer. Place the Flash MP3 player and the download link near each other so visitors can choose. Third, consider adding the MP3 file to a podcast. One huge advantage of using MP3 is that the same files can be used for progressive download as well as for downloading and playing.

Video

Video is commonly played using progressive download just as audio is. Another approach used to deliver video or sometimes audio is streaming. People often refer to progressive download as streaming; however, the two are not quite the same. Streaming requires a streaming server—a web server with additional streaming software that orchestrates the download of media content. A streaming server communicates with a plug-in in a browser and attempts to maximize the quality over the current connection. The advantage of streaming is that downloaded data can be dynamically adjusted prior to and as the file plays. For example, if the connection starts out fast but then slows down for some reason, the software on the streaming server can automatically reduce the amount of data sent. This reduces the quality but can allow the stream to continue without pausing. For video, a streaming server may continue to send the same audio stream but remove many of the frames of the video. So the audio plays normally, but the display appears jerky due to the missing frames. Of course, frames can be added and quality can be improved if the connection improves. Streaming servers can also support jumping into a latter part of the prerecorded file quickly without downloading the first part of the file. Another advantage of streaming is that streaming software can support live streaming. Like live television, live streaming is transmitting audio or video as it is captured with only a short delay. With live streaming, one computer usually captures audio or video and sends it to the streaming server on the internet. The streaming server then sends the live stream out to visitors shortly after it is received.

Streaming, especially live streaming, is an exciting technology, but for the majority of churches, I do not recommend live streaming mainly because the internet has an on-demand culture. Website visitors are less willing to figure out time-zone differences and to work to visit your website at a specific time in order to see a live event. A better solution is usually to record a version that can be posted shortly after the event and can remain on the website for visitors to access any time they choose. Additionally, events can contain copyrighted material or various mishaps such as equipment failures or a temporary power outage. Cutting out or replacing sections of the event is fairly easy if it was prerecorded, but is much more difficult if the event is broadcast live. With a live stream, you are forced to edit and replace as needed as the event is happening. Finally, live streaming requires a lot of technology all working together reliably in order to succeed. It requires highly reliable equipment to capture and process the stream, excellent internet connectivity to send the stream from the source to the streaming server, one or more streaming servers that can be costly, and sufficient server bandwidth for all the simultaneous media streams. Bringing all these together for live streaming can be technically challenging to set up and operate, and it is costly. We know this well because the Web-Empowered Church Team helps conduct live streaming events.

Despite its challenges, a streaming server has some nice features and can be a useful ministry tool in specific instances. For example, we have seen live streaming work well for Baptist state conventions and United Methodist annual conferences to allow hundreds of members of those organizations to watch the proceedings live. Also, some churches now broadcast their worship experience either live or prerecorded at specific times. The United Methodist Church of the Resurrection in Leawood, Kansas, is an example of a web-empowered church that streams its entire worship events with great ministry success.

A technology referred to as "Cloud Computing" can be helpful for those who want to stream events live or rebroadcast recorded events at specific times. Cloud computing services can be purchased from companies like Amazon and Google with large numbers of servers that are spread geographically and have very high-speed internet connections. These servers have special cloud computing software on them that allows them to appear as any number of virtual servers that are also very flexible to configure and can be rapidly deployed. The cloud can work well for media streaming because many virtual servers can be deployed on demand to provide the streams needed to serve the current visitors. Using cloud computing is often more cost effective than having your own streaming servers or paying a media streaming company because virtual servers in the cloud can be configured, put online, and taken offline very quickly, and you only pay for the time you use them.

As with audio, there are many video formats from which to choose. The most popular video formats used on websites include Audio Video Interleave (AVI), Moving Picture Experts Group (MPEG), QuickTime (MOV), Windows Media Video (WMV), and Flash Video (FLV). Based on the video capture/editor software you are using, your initial video files will probably be in AVI, WMV, MPEG, or MOV format. As with graphics, you should initially store the video files in the common format used by your video capture program to maintain quality and to facilitate modifying them in the future. Also, each video file format has its own special mathematical technique, or "codec" (coder-decoder), for compressing video. Converting video from one codec to another can result in loss of quality due to interference between the codecs. It is best to stay with one main format while you edit and then convert it to the final web format when you are ready to post the video on the web. There are a few acceptable formats for web video, but I believe that MPEG-4 is currently the best choice for adding video to your website and for video podcasting. Previously we used and recommended FLV for websites, and it continues to work well, but MPEG-4 technology has matured and appears to be best for the future. It also plays on smart phones. What follows is some basic information about these common formats.

AVI: AVI is a common capture format, so your files may start as AVI files. AVI files are often very large and may not play on all computers because of different codecs required to view them. AVI is not recommended for posting on a website.

MOV: MOV is Apple Computer's QuickTime format. QuickTime can support streaming or progressive download. It is also sometimes used for video podcasting. As expected,

QuickTime works well on a Macintosh computer. For Windows users, the biggest challenge with QuickTime is that the download installation file for the QuickTime plug-in is quite large, over 30 megabytes. People with dial-up connections find it difficult to download; they sometimes just give up. Also, the QuickTime plug-in can be intrusive by setting itself as a default player and generating too many informational pop-ups. I do not recommend using the MOV format.

WMV: WMV is Microsoft's video format. For Microsoft Windows users it is preinstalled and works well. Getting and installing plug-ins for non-Microsoft-based computers is challenging. The plug-ins are now free but must be installed, and they are not always kept up-to-date. WMV supports streaming, and the streaming server comes with the latest version of Microsoft Windows server software. The Windows server software is fairly expensive, but it supports video streaming, including live streaming. One key advantage of WMV is that computer users who are already running Windows have the basic tools needed to edit and produce video. Due to the popularity of Windows and the availability of the tools, I consider WMV a viable solution. And if you specifically need live streaming, WMV is probably the least expensive solution.

FLV: FLV is a popular web video format. The FLV format can support both streaming and progressive download. In order to stream FLV files, you will need the Adobe streaming server or a similar streaming media server. Unfortunately, streaming media servers tend to be expensive. The biggest advantage of the FLV format is that it can play inside a webpage using the popular Flash browser plug-in. The way FLV files play is a little different from other video formats, because other video plug-ins usually only play video. But Flash is more general purpose and supports animation, audio, and video. A Flash movie plays the FLV, and the Flash movie is like any other common Flash movie, except that it includes Flash-provided features to do progressive downloading and to play an FLV file. This different way of playing video opens up some interesting possibilities. For example, you could develop a custom Flash movie that is the FLV player for your website. Or you could embed the FLV within a Flash animation sequence. In other words, you can display the FLV anywhere and at any point in the Flash movie.

You do not need to create Flash movies in order to create and play FLV files. Several free Flash movie FLV players are already available. If you use one, make sure it supports progressive downloading—not all of them do. As you work with FLV files, note that since FLV files require a Flash movie to play them, they may not play on your local computer when you click them. If this happens, you can search for "standalone FLV player" on the web to find, download, and install a free standalone FLV player. FLV remains a useful and viable format for online video.

MPEG: MPEG-1 and MPEG-2 are usually too large for viewing with streaming or progressive download; however, MPEG-4 is highly compressed and can play online in a Flash player or can be distributed via a podcast. Video podcasting is implemented like audio podcasting but uses MPEG-4 video files instead of MP3 audio files. In general, video podcasts are less popular than audio podcasts, probably because video podcasting is newer. The video files can be quite large to transfer and store, and some portable media players cannot display video or MPEG-4 video specifically. However, video podcasting is worth considering, especially if your organization is already producing video.

As you can see, the big advantage of selecting Flash as a universal plug-in to support animation, audio, and video is that visitors need only one main plug-in. And that plug-in is one of the most popular of all plug-ins. Over the years we have endured the challenges of multiple special and changing plug-ins. Meeting these challenges was not pleasant at times, and the options will probably change again with HTML5. However, we are currently pleased with using Flash as our universal plug-in when HTML alone is not sufficient, and I expect that you will be as well.

CHAPTER 8

Constructing Your Website

Hosting your website, website creation tools, and guidelines

I remember when we created our thousandth webpage. What an achievement! Within a few months, some of the staff suggested we do a complete redesign of the website. What a great idea! Little did we know how much work that would entail.

When our church internet ministry had been going strong for three years, the entire team was still made up of unpaid servants. We had at least one thousand HTML files because we had not yet reached the era of CMS (content management software). We had hundreds of graphics files and a few hundred video and audio files. When the staff from our church came to me and suggested that we do a redesign to give our website a fresh look and feel, I agreed that this was a great idea. Of course, there was one minor detail. OK, it was a major detail. The complete look and feel of our website was stored over and over in each of the one thousand HTML files. In each file, we faithfully reproduced the banner across the top, the footer along the bottom, the buttons in the button bar, the copyright notice, the paragraph title styles, the fonts—everything. And, worse yet, most of the pages were created by hand, so even though they looked the same, the underlying HTML was often surprisingly different. The inconsistencies made it far more difficult to write programs that could read these files and automatically change the look and feel.

To this day, we are recovering from many of our past decisions as we continue to update and enhance our website at an increasing pace. We have certainly had our share of mistakes along the way, but in this chapter I will share what we have found to be the best practices for creating and maintaining an excellent ministry-based website.

We Need a Heavenly Website Host

Before you look for a place to host your website, know what your hosting needs are. Start by choosing a CMS, because a CMS often has specific hosting requirements and you can quickly rule out options that would not support your CMS. Next, identify special features you need, such as supporting many email accounts or serving many large audio or video files. Fortunately, most packages that can host a CMS come with the other features you will need. Finally, as you compare packages, be sure to look for the frequency of backups. Really cheap hosting may not include any backups, and that is not good. A backup is a copy of your data made to a tape or another hard drive; it is used to recover from a hard drive failure or an accidental file or data deletion. One thing you can count on is that 100 percent of all hard drives will fail eventually. Nightly backups are best.

Web-Hosting Application Service Providers (ASPs): Some CMS software is available only from specific web-hosting ASPs (this is also known as "Software as a Service"). "ASP" refers to a mode of business in which the ASP organization supplies online services that allow remote use of special ASP-owned software running on ASP-owned computers. Web-hosting ASPs can be ministries or commercial companies, so costs can range from no cost to quite expensive. Web-hosting ASPs run their own custom CMS, and users do not have access to the CMS software. Most web-hosting ASPs provide packages that include their CMS and various other hosting options such as email and data backups. If you choose a CMS from a web-hosting ASP, you have automatically selected your hosting arrangement. Some churches like this because many of the details are handled for them. Also, web-hosting ASPs commonly provide an array of website templates and can usually develop custom templates for a fee. Some specialize in hosting church websites and provide special features that churches need. Most advertise themselves as easy to use, and many live up to that claim. Using a web-hosting ASP is a way to get your church on the web with a professional-looking website very quickly. Web-hosting ASPs are a quick and easy way to handle the technical details of getting your church on the internet. If you plan to use a web-hosting ASP, consider the following suggestions:

1. Sometimes these services limit the growth of your web ministry. For example, you may want to add interactive features, databases, email lists, audio, or video. Be sure the web-hosting ASP has adequate growth options. Pay attention to limitations of all types such as bandwidth, disk space, numbers of accounts, and numbers of pages.
2. Adding features such as increasing network capacity and disk space can be expensive relative to the initial package. Verify that growth options you might need are affordable.
3. Think about how you might move your website content to a different hosting arrangement in the future. Even if the web-hosting ASP provides great service today, it is unlikely that you will host with this company forever. Things change. People change. Financial situations change. Organizations come and go and merge with others. Moving a website can be painfully difficult. Since you will not have access to the CMS software owned by the ASP, find out if it has any methods of extracting the content from your website to help you move it to a new location. Automated methods are not common, and the usual solution is to

spend many hours manually copying the content and files to your new location.

4. Look for copyrighted features such as templates or graphics. Also look for proprietary applications to which the ASP may claim intellectual property rights. If you move your website in the future, you cannot take these with you unless you get permission from the ASP, and permission may be impossible or costly to obtain.

I have worked with a few churches that chose to use web-hosting ASPs and had beautiful templates. They used the templates for years, and the website look became their church brand. When they decided to move their website, they learned that the template they used was copyrighted and could not be used elsewhere. They felt like their template was being held for ransom, and they were very upset about it. But because the ASP owned the template, there was nothing they could do except create a new template at their new location.

Web-hosting ASPs are not evil. They typically have huge investments in their custom CMS software and the other features they provide. They need to protect that investment to stay in business. They also help churches because they offer a fast and easy way to get started. You need to understand the relationship and choose based upon your own needs.

Commercial and Open-Source CMS: There are numerous choices for commercial and open-source CMS software. It is not possible to list and compare them all here because there are so many and they change so frequently, but you can find more information by searching the web. Some of the things we considered when approaching this decision for the Web-Empowered Church are God's provision, content entry, multilingual capacity, dynamic content, extension installation, templates, hosting options, cost, powerful capability, and extensive support. Based on these, we chose TYPO3 as our CMS. For an explanation of how TYPO3 addresses each of these criteria, please see chapter 12.

When considering non-ASP solutions, once you choose a CMS that appears to meet your needs, you can look at its hosting requirements. Server requirements may be listed as Windows, WAMP, or LAMP. If the CMS requires ASP.NET server-side scripting, the web server should be a standard Windows Server running the Microsoft Windows Server operating system, internet Information Server (IIS) Web Server, and SQL Server database. WAMP-configured servers run the Windows operating system, an Apache Web Server, a MySQL database, and PHP (which is usually included in Apache). Notice that the first letters from each software component form the acronym "WAMP." The LAMP configuration is like the WAMP configuration, but the operating system is Linux instead of Windows. TYPO3 installs and runs best on LAMP-configured servers. The CMS will also have requirements for memory and disk space. As a rule of thumb, more memory is always better, and disk space should be checked more carefully if you plan to use a lot of audio or video. Hosting details can be a bit confusing. If you are unsure about requirements or features, ask your prospective hosting company about hosting your desired CMS.

Once you know the configuration of your server, there are some additional options to consider. You can choose to host your website on a shared server, a virtual private server, a dedicated server, or a collocated server. Here is a brief description of the differences:

1. **Shared Server**—this type of server hosts many websites, including yours, on the same server computer.
2. **Virtual Private Server (VPS)**—a VPS runs on a server computer inside special virtualizing software that makes the VPS appear like an actual separate server computer. Multiple VPS can run on a single physical server computer. This rather unique technique is very popular and useful for server management and is the basis for cloud computing. Your website runs alone within the VPS.

3. **Dedicated Server**—your website is on a server computer that is dedicated to your web ministry. A dedicated-server hosting plan usually includes server management services.
4. **Collocated Server**—your website is on your own server computer located at a hosting company. Normally you assume full management responsibility for it.

Fortunately, for most organizations, a shared server, also known as "shared hosting," is a good choice. Shared hosting is less expensive, and most organization websites do not need all the resources of other server types. Most websites on the internet are hosted on shared servers, and most web-hosting ASPs offer only shared hosting. One potential issue with shared hosting is that the hosting company may put too many websites on one server, which can result in sluggish performance or memory errors. In addition, it is possible for any of the websites on the server to run scripts that slow down the entire server. The quality of shared hosting service can vary but is not typically a significant issue. If you are unsure, begin with shared hosting because you can always move to another option later.

If costs are less of an issue and especially if you plan to add a lot of audio and video, then I recommend starting with a managed VPS. One advantage of a VPS is that other websites hosted on the same computer should have no effect on the responsiveness of your website. In the early years of the Ginghamsburg internet ministry, our website was on a shared server, and it worked well for us. We later moved to a dedicated server and now to a VPS running on our own server computer.

Self-hosting is also an option. With self-hosting, you host your website on a computer at your location or in someone's home or perhaps a local small business. The challenge with this approach is providing reliable service to your visitors. Visitors expect a website to be accessible twenty-four hours a day, so it is important to host where the internet connectivity is extremely reliable and where backup power is available. Most hosting companies have multiple redundant connections to the internet to reduce network outages, and they have backup generators that keep computers running when electrical power fails. Also, most hosting companies provide additional services such as monitoring the networks for hacker activity, offering 24/7 support, creating backups, and making security updates. These services can be time consuming to perform, and they often require special expertise. Unless you have unique hosting capabilities, it is usually best to host with a fully equipped hosting company instead. Due to network reliability concerns and costs, we have never seriously considered self-hosting our church's websites.

Choosing a hosting company is difficult. There are many options, and until you use a company's hosting you really don't know for sure the quality and service you will receive. Here are a few items to consider when choosing a hosting company:

1. **Free Hosting:** We greatly appreciate ministries that provide free hosting. They have paved the way for more organizations to get online. However, if you want to truly web empower your ministries, you are likely to quickly outgrow these hosting services. Many of them are not able to host a CMS like TYPO3 because it uses too many web server resources, and they must host and support many websites at a very low cost.

2. **Paid Hosting:** It is probably not a good idea to use hosting packages that cost $5 or less per month unless they are subsidized in some way. Realistically, $5 per month is probably not enough income to cover the costs for the server and support or to ensure that the server is not overloaded. Excellent shared hosting is worth at least $1 per day, or about $30 per month. As your church becomes web empowered, your website will likely more than pay for itself through reduced paper and mailing costs. Try not to make cost the dominant deciding factor when you choose a hosting company.

3. **Ask for Advice:** As with other services, it is helpful to ask people where they host their websites and if they are pleased. Larger hosting companies can often provide more features at a lower cost, but service can be limited. Local hosting companies can provide personal service, but may get overloaded. You need to shop for a hosting company and find a hosting package that fits your needs. You always have the option to move to another hosting company at a later date.

The Ginghamsburg Church websites and the Web-Empowered Church (WEC) websites are hosted by WEC itself. Hosting your church or ministry website with WEC directly helps the WEC ministry. Hosting at WEC includes installation of and ongoing updates to the WEC Starter Package, which includes TYPO3.

Adding Other Online Services

Most web ministries today will have other components in addition to the main website that provide additional features. That could be a feature as simple as integrating a Google calendar into your main website, or it could be an external website hosted at an online service like Facebook or Twitter. These services will be discussed more in the following chapter.

You may need to register for multiple accounts to accommodate multiple target audiences such as one for adults and one for youth. Fortunately, you don't need to find a host for these services because part of their service includes hosting on their server computers. But you need to go to each of these services to register one or more accounts. For many services it can be a bit confusing because the services are often oriented toward individual people registering for accounts and not organizations registering. In addition, registering is not hard, but if you are using multiple services, then it can get a bit confusing to keep track of all the accounts and who on your team has access. It is good to think ahead about who will be maintaining these websites and how they will be accessing them. You will need to coordinate with your team to determine what usernames and passwords are to be used for the different systems, and you should change passwords when team members leave or change roles. We have had some success with using one common email address (InternetTeam@YourChurchName.org) for the main email account supplied to each of these services during registration. If you need multiple email addresses when registering multiple accounts on one service, then you can create additional email addresses and forward to the main address. That main email address is actually an email list that sends emails to each of the leaders on the team. In fact, we do this for our domain name registrations and our hosting accounts as well. It ensures that the team receives any critical messages from any service we use like "your domain name is ready to expire" or "the service will be down for maintenance." And the email list can be changed as the team changes without changing the registered email address at each service.

When you register, it is important to choose usernames that match your organization's name instead of that of the person registering. This is important because the links to the website and the page content are likely to use that name. A longer descriptive name can usually work well for these accounts because it is rare that visitors will type the account name since the websites will usually be accessed from your main website or added to a friends list. Also, longer names are less likely to be taken. As with the name, for services that require just one account, the information like the address and phone number should be information for your organization, and not that of a specific person.

Development Tools

The tools you use to develop your website depend on personal preference and the computer you are using. Most of your team should not need to purchase anything. The types of tools you may need include:

Browsers: It is important to have multiple popular web browsers on your computer to test pages and ensure that they display correctly in different browsers. Examples include: Internet Explorer and Mozilla Firefox.

HTML/CSS Editor: In the past, a what-you-see-is-what-you-get (WYSIWYG) editor was the most critical tool for anyone creating websites. These editors helped develop HTML, CSS, and JavaScript. However, most people who use a CMS do not need a WYSIWYG editor. I used a WYSIWYG editor almost daily for many years, but now that our websites are all in a CMS, I don't have need for one because the rich text editor displays right inside my browser. WYSIWYG editors remain useful tools for advanced web developers, template designers, and server-side scripting developers. One example of an HTML or CSS editor is Dreamweaver.

Programmer's Text Editor: All computers come with a basic text file editor installed, but website developers commonly use more powerful text editors that include features like tabs for editing multiple files at a time, color highlighting of tags and keywords, and advanced "find and replace" features. Getting a programmer's text editor is optional, and you can add this tool at any time. Examples of text editors include NoteTab Light, UltraEdit, and TextMate.

Graphics Editor: A basic graphics editor is an important program for most web developers. The key features include cropping, resizing, adjusting color and brightness, and saving in the JPG or GIF format. All computers come with a basic graphics file editor installed, and these tools may serve the need. Serious graphics designers, however, need much more capable graphics editors. Examples of graphics editors include PaintShop Pro, Adobe Photoshop, or Photoshop Elements, and GIMP.

Audio or Video Editor/Encoder/Player: If you plan to include audio or video on your website, you will need software (and possibly hardware) to capture and edit the audio or video. Depending on the software you are using to capture and edit, you may need additional software to encode files into different formats. You may also need an audio or video player. Some or all of these tools are likely to be already available on your computer. For most web applications, you will need only basic editing tools, but the features you need depend on your capability and the output you desire. Examples of video editing software include Windows Movie Maker and Adobe Premiere.

Flash: If you plan to edit or create Flash movies, you will need Adobe Flash. It is not required if you only plan to use Flash video but not create it. One example of a current Flash program is Adobe Flash Builder.

Word Processing: Website content commonly arrives in a Word-formatted document, so it is usually important to have word processing capability to extract the content. Examples of word processing programs include Microsoft Word and OpenOffice.

Spellcheck: A spell check that can check the spelling of fields in a web form is a very useful tool, especially when a CMS supports entry of content into web forms. One example of a spell check program is Google Toolbar.

File Transfer and Remote Shell: In most cases, your website administrators will need tools to securely log on to your web server and to transfer files. Some of these tools may already be on your computer. Some examples of such tools include PuTTY, Remote Desktop, and WS_FTP.

Email, Instant Messenger: You will want to communicate among web team members. Two useful tools are email and instant messaging. Again, it is likely that you already have these on your computer for other reasons. Examples of email and instant messaging programs include Microsoft Outlook, AOL AIM, Trillian, Yoono, and Skype.

Don't Create a Mess

Before you get started with your developmental tools, it is important to do some planning. Even for a simple website, the files and directories can quickly become a mess. When we started putting our pastor's sermons online in text format, we created a folder called "sermon" to store the sermon graphics. Each weekly sermon had about eight graphics associated with it. After a year and a half, the folder contained more than five hundred graphics files, which made listing the files very sluggish. We realized that we could not have just one sermon folder for all graphics because it would end up with thousands of files in it. We now have one sermon folder per year. We also came up with a way to name our sermon graphics files based on the date of the Sunday that they were preached. The names looked like this: "apr1007a.jpg," "apr1007b.jpg," and "dec1407a.jpg." In order to ensure that you can find files on your growing website, have at least a general plan for where to store different files. The plan needs to be something that makes sense to all the people creating your website. We base most folder names on the names of the sections of the website. For example, we have an "About Us" section on our website, so we have an "aboutus" folder where we store files associated with the "About Us" section. The "aboutus" folder has a subfolder called "staff," where the staff pictures are stored. This approach makes sense to our team. For periodically generated files like sermons and newsletters, we add the year to the end of the folder name. For example, we have folders "sermon00" and "sermon01" for sermon files for the years 2000 and 2001, respectively. Filenames can also become confusing unless they have some consistency. For files associated with a date—like a monthly newsletter, an audio sermon, or the weekly bulletin—include the date in the filename. For example, you could use the format

"YYYYMMDD" where YYYY is the year, MM is the two-digit number of the month (with a leading "0" if needed), and DD is the two-digit day (with leading "0" if needed). Following this format, "b20110128.pdf" or "bulletin012811.pdf" could be the weekly bulletin file for January 28, 2011. The advantage of this approach is that the files sort chronologically and it is easy to find a file for any specific week. Our experience has shown that most files are associated with periodic dates.

Always be on the lookout for ways to do things in organized and consistent ways. For example, store CSS styles only in specific files and places where you can manage them. When you are in a hurry to solve a formatting problem, it is easy to add a little CSS to fix the specific formatting issue. The problem comes later when you want to make global changes to the styles. Thinking long-term is best because the long term will be here eventually.

Helping Search Engines Find You

As I explained in chapter 4, the three main ways to bring visitors to your website are (1) promote it within and around your church, (2) register on websites that list churches, and (3) register your web address in order for search engines to find it. There are a few other things you can do to your website that will help search engines incorporate your website contents into their search indexes.

Search engines, such as Google and Yahoo!, run special programs called "spiders," "crawlers," or "search bots" that browse websites, capture their pages, and index the words in the pages. This huge index is used to generate search results. The results are links to websites that match the visitor's search criteria. Spider programs run constantly. In order to avoid slowing websites down with many simultaneous requests, most spider programs request a few pages at a time and spread requests over time. Of course, they must return to your website again and again to see if any changes have been made. As you might guess, this is quite a mammoth task given the millions of websites on the internet. Webpage creators can make it easier for these programs to "crawl" our websites, which in turn boosts our presence in the results lists.

Search engines rank results lists according to a measure of relevance. The goal is to have the most relevant and useful websites (based on the search criteria) listed first. High search engine ranking can mean high profits, so search engine companies keep private the details of the techniques they use to decide ranking, and they are constantly refining these techniques. Website developers work hard to get their websites ranked more highly. The process of trying to attain high search engine ranking is called "search engine optimization" (SEO). There are websites and books that teach SEO and even SEO businesses that help companies increase their rankings. For Christian organizations and other nonprofits, hiring someone is probably not affordable or necessary. Here are a few tips that will help you address the most critical SEO needs:

1. Focus on creating a website with a lot of well-organized and useful content. Great websites naturally provide many good words that search engines will index.
2. Ensure that your website is standard XHTML so that search engines will understand and index the pages correctly.
3. Encourage other respectable websites to link to your website. Search engines consider these links to be a "vote" for your website.
4. Think of the types of words visitors might use to look for your website, and include those words in the content of your webpages. Note that spider software cannot read words in graphics or in Flash, so it is best not to use graphics to display important words and titles.
5. Include an alternate-text tag that describes each graphic. Search engines index the content of these alternate-text tags. Avoid hidden text and links because the search engine may consider them deceptive.

6. Avoid using a CMS that cannot create standard-looking URLs. Standard URLs are made up of a domain, some number of directories separated by slashes, an optional file-name, and optional parameters—for example, http://Domain.org/aboutus/staff. Most CMS systems generate all pages using one main script file. From a search engine's perspective, all the pages on the website appear to be one page with parameters sent to it—for example, http://Domain.org/index.php?id=2 ("2" identifies the page). The TYPO3 CMS supports standard URLs, so it works well with search engines.

7. Add some basic meta tags to your pages. Meta tags provide additional information about your website and its contents, but do not display on a webpage in a browser. Meta tags are placed between the start and end of the head tag (between <head> and </head>). They are usually formatted like this: <meta name="NameAttribute" content="the content of the meta tag"/>, where NameAttribute is a predefined name or one that you created. The most valuable predefined meta tag name attributes are probably "description" and "key-words." Using "description," you provide a short descrip-tion of the website or page. Using "keywords," you provide a list of keywords for the page. Here is an example: <meta name="keywords" content="Christian, Church, Jesus"/>. Feel free to use many keywords. Use each word only one time, and include both singular and plural versions if visi-tors might enter either as a search word. TYPO3 provides support for automated meta tag generation.

Website Statistics

Once your website is up and running, the obvious questions are *How many people are coming to the website?* and *Which pages are they viewing?* Most web servers have log files where every "hit" (web-server transaction) is recorded. Information logged includes (1) the type of request, (2) the file/page requested, (3) parameters that were exchanged, (4) the previous page the visitor was browsing, and (5) the date and time. The log also includes visitor information such as (1) browser type, (2) IP address, (3) computer type, (4) operating system, and (5) other computer settings. There is a wealth of information in the log, but the concept of hits is not very meaningful. A visitor browsing a webpage will generate any number of hits depending on the files needed to display the page, including all graphics files. Browser cache adds to the confusion because sometimes a browser will use a cached version of a file, and that will not generate a hit. So the logs contain many details, but the log file information in its raw form is not very valuable.

Web servers usually come with web-log analysis ("stats") software that processes the log files. TYPO3 supports creation and analysis of logs using a popular open-source program called AWStats or Google Analytics. A stats program summarizes the log files and provides some extremely useful information. For example, the stats show how many times a specific page was requested. The webpage creator really doesn't know if a visitor stopped to read the page or not, only that the web server received the request and sent out the page. This information is still helpful because it tells which pages on the website are most popular. The stats program will usually help by listing the pages in order of popularity. Stats use the logged computer IP address and lookups on the internet to figure out visitors' internet service providers and even the countries from which they are visiting. This is how we know that people from more than eighty different countries visit the Ginghamsburg website each month. The log files also contain computer type, operating system, and browser type. So the stats provide quite a bit of visitor information.

You might have noticed that I do not say how many different people visit a website. It is not possible to compute that directly from the stats information; however, Google Analytics does attempt to statistically estimate that number. The most accurate and useful measurement is to count visits. A visit is an occasion when a person who comes to the website browses one or more pages and then leaves. If she or he leaves and comes back fifteen minutes or more later, then that is counted as another visit. Using a combination of information in the logs, the stats program can estimate visits fairly accurately. Visits from search engine spiders are ignored in the process. Most web administrators use visits as the primary measure of traffic to their websites. When I am backed into a corner and must provide an estimate of the number of different human visitors coming to the website, I use the number that comes from Google Analytics. Please note that Google Analytics requires one to register with Google and set up the account to include special JavaScript on each webpage, but it provides one with useful statistics, including various graphs.

I encourage you to experiment with your stats software. You can look at the information in so many different ways, and it is fun to play with and to think about. At Ginghamsburg, I report key information to our staff leadership and to the internet ministry team each month. It helps us all get a better understanding of the impact of our ministry and which features are most popular. Over the years it has been exciting to see our visits increase from ten to one hundred to over one thousand per day. It is great to have a tool that can help us monitor progress, and it is a real blessing to know that people are benefiting from our efforts. We are blessed to serve.

Keeping It Going and Growing

Creating an excellent internet ministry is more about perseverance than brilliance. It is important to think of your internet ministry as an ongoing long-term ministry and not as a project to create a website. Projects can be completed; ministries are never completed. If you stick with it, your internet ministry can grow over time to enhance the other ministries in your organization as they each add a web component. The internet is not going to decline; it will only get bigger and more pervasive throughout all aspects of our lives and the life of the church. We need to embrace it and to grow and adapt as it grows and adapts because it is an increasingly vital tool for ministry.

CHAPTER 9

Using Free Online Services

Using Facebook, YouTube, Twitter, Skype, Google, and More

What an amazing opportunity the church has to connect with people! Hundreds of millions of people around the world are using social networking websites like Facebook and MySpace, posting video and photos on websites like YouTube and Flickr, creating blogs on websites like Blogger and WordPress, and messaging via services like Twitter. Worldwide internet usage has moved from an information focus to a people-connection focus, and, fortunately, people connection is what the church is all about. Whether we are evangelizing, teaching, or caring for people, we are connecting with people and helping them connect with God. This offers a unique opportunity for the church to expand its impact. We must learn how best to use these powerful tools for ministry and then use them to reach the world.

Matthew 28:19 says, "Go therefore and make disciples of all nations." This principle of going into the world to minister and to disciple is a clear mandate in Scripture. It is the Great Commission. Social networking provides a wonderful opportunity for us to go into the world. Social networking can best be thought of as a wonderful mission field. In our planning and overall approach it is valuable to think of the internet as a mission field like any other physical mission field in the world.

If you were going to design the perfect mission field, what would it be? You might describe it as being:

- a place filled with millions of unsaved and accessible people.
- a place where people openly, regularly, and publicly share their opinions, thoughts, feelings, concerns, fears, and needs without any prompting.
- a place where people connect with other people in community, and where people like and expect to meet new people.
- a place where many people provide a picture and a little information about themselves so you can know a little about them before you communicate with them.
- a place where it is OK to be creative, different, and simply yourself.
- a place where people openly debate, discuss, and exchange ideas, including spiritual matters.
- a place where people like to go and hang out—a place that is fun, sometimes silly, and where people smile and laugh.
- a place that is close to home so we can get there quickly when we have time, without immunizations, passports, or plane trips. And it would all be free.
- a safe place without danger or evil influences.

Except for the last characteristic, which can't happen in a fruitful mission field (and we'll discuss how to exercise caution a little later), this perfect mission field exists right now. It exists on the internet in public online services that connect people in community: social networking, social media, blogs, chat rooms, video sharing, photo sharing, and discussion groups.

The internet is a uniquely fertile and accessible mission field. And recognizing it as such means there are several things to keep in mind.

Learn the Language and Culture: The internet has its own language, culture, and customs. For example, "lol" means laughing out loud. It can also mean that I acknowledge what you are saying. DID YOU KNOW THAT TYPING IN ALL CAPITAL LETTERS IS VERY RUDE AND CONSIDERED YELLING? In the online world it is. The online community can quickly spot an outsider, so as in other mission fields, it is important to learn the language, culture, and customs before you can be an effective missionary there.

Prepare for the Dangers: We need to recognize that the places on the internet where we are going as missionaries can be dangerous and filled with evil influences. I recently spent some time exploring this mission field by visiting numerous personal home pages and just following the links they provided. During this time I saw more evil than I had seen on the internet in the last several years. As I thought and prayed about it, I became increasingly saddened by it all. So many people are lost, confused, hurting, and in need of Jesus. I challenge you, and myself, to begin evangelizing in this way. The time I spent learning was emotionally draining, but I know in my heart this is where we need to be.

Go: We must go to them. Christians have tried to put church online or to build evangelistic websites where people can come and meet Jesus. We have seen some small successes, but that is a bit like building a church in the suburbs and wondering why people from the inner city do not come. We can learn from mission ministry more than we might expect. As with other missions, we should identify, equip, and send missionaries into the places where the people are and can best be reached. We need to go to them. As you plan and grow your internet ministry, I encourage you to consider sending out missionaries to the internet, using online services. The mission field is plentiful. We just need to go.

So Where Are the People Going?

The most popular public websites have some way to connect socially with other people. "Friends" or "buddy" lists often show each person his or her many social connections, which could be family, friends, coworkers, organizations, and so forth. Some of these websites promote meeting new people, and most include the ability to post comments. Most of these websites are also accessible on smart phones such as Windows Mobile, Android, and iPhone, or an iPad. Due to the limited processing power of cell phones and the limited screen space, the interfaces are greatly simplified when displayed on a cell phone, but the core features of the service remain accessible.

Below is a description of some of the more popular categories of free online services that you may want to use in your web ministry. This list is not meant to be comprehensive, and online services change rapidly; so always be watching for other new developments and opportunities. It is an exciting time for online ministry. At the same time, I caution you to try to make sure your church's main features appear on your home page as much as possible to keep it simple for your visitors instead of forcing them to jump from website to website to enjoy your web ministry. We'll talk about specific ministry uses for these services in later chapters.

Social Networking: Popular social networking websites like Facebook and MySpace include friends lists, but also help you keep in touch by notifying you of what others have recently shared, including status updates, blog posts, photos, music, videos, and more. It really is a wonderful way to stay connected. My wife and I are part of a large extended family that includes many nieces and nephews with whom we want to stay in touch. It is amazing how easy it is to know how they are doing in school and various life activities. For the young marrieds we love to see the baby photos, too. And it allows their uncle Mark to jump in and offer a bit of uncle advice and support now and then even though we may go months without seeing each other. Those of us in web ministry need to watch these websites closely for additional ministry opportunities and creative ways we can use these tools for ministry. These websites are continuously evolving and adding new features in an attempt to keep people coming back. Of course, like television, they are funded mainly from advertising revenue, so their main purpose is to develop features that encourage everyone to visit as often as possible and for as long as possible (what we sometimes call "sticky" websites). A recent trend for these websites has been offering social games that must be tended to over and over. If you come up with a great way to use one of these features in ministry, please send me an email so we can share it with others (see chapter 13 for my contact information). These website developers are using their creative gifts from God to create powerful social networking tools, so let's use our creative gifts to use those tools for Kingdom work.

Social Media: Social media websites like YouTube, Tangle (a Christian site), Vimeo, and Flickr enable visitors to post their own creations on the internet in the form of videos (YouTube, Tangle, Vimeo) and photos (Flickr). Visitors can rate or comment on the media, or they can view other related media. Some churches use YouTube or similar systems to store video since storage is free and the video can be embedded in a normal web page. That can work well, although in the case of YouTube, this results in a link to the YouTube site. Unfortunately, there are temptations on YouTube that can take people in an unhealthy direction. So I recommend not using YouTube for main video storage or to embed videos in your site. If possible, it is usually best to keep all resources (webpages and media) on one website because it simplifies updates, and it improves reliability by not requiring that several servers all work together to deliver one page, such as a sermons page.

The greatest ministry power of YouTube is probably the potential for a viral video. A "viral" video is one that becomes extremely popular and ends up being viewed by many—even millions—people. Some viral videos even end up on TV for free. Creating a truly viral video is difficult, but posting highly creative videos there can become a significant ministry in itself. If you do any sort of generally applicable and creative video at your church, I encourage you to post it on social media websites. I am not sure of the full ministry value, but our staff created a rap video about giving to our New Path food pantry. It really was very well done. The internet ministry team posted it on multiple social media websites. It got quite a few visitors and attracted some attention. I am not sure any lives were changed by that particular video, but there are a lot worse things people could be watching.

Blogging: Blogger and WordPress are two popular places to get quick and free online blogs. They host the blogs for you and take care of all the details. However, for an organization's official blog or its leaders' blogs, I suggest hosting them on your main website. The four reasons for doing this are (1) it is more user friendly for visitors to go to fewer websites, (2) you can ensure that you won't have unwanted ads appearing on your blog at some point in the future, (3) the pages fit in better with the appearance of your website, and (4) it simplifies site maintenance and data entry. As I mentioned earlier, even if you blog using a social networking website, there is still significant value in having the main source of the blog with the visitors' comments on your main website. For Ginghamsburg, we created a separate website for our pastor that contains his blog. We created a separate website because it has a different target audience that goes beyond our church attendees to include other ministry leaders who read his books or hear him speak at conferences and workshops.

It sometimes seems like everyone has a personal blog in some form, and this can be an issue with staff and ministry leaders who represent the organization to the public. If a lot of ministry-related communication is going on within a personal blog, it is probably best to create another blog just for that purpose and to host it on the organization's website. Personal blogs naturally tend to include a mix of posts about family, work, hobbies, and life in general. They also tend to be a place where people freely express themselves even to the point of complaining, venting, or sharing private information. As a result, bloggers can occasionally forget who is following their blog. We hear news stories of people being fired from their jobs for sharing information on their blogs that hurts the company they work for. Ginghamsburg can't normally require that one's personal blog be hosted on our main website, and it probably does not even make sense to ask that it be done this way. But it is important to remind leaders who blog that they need to always keep in mind that they represent the organization to the public, and the public is reading what they write, viewing the photos they post, and judging them and the organization based on those entries. I have talked to several active bloggers and to my surprise, most of them admit blogging something that they wished they could take back or that resulted in them getting in some sort of unneeded conflict. It is important to remind your leaders of this situation and to remind them to take responsibility for what they put on their blogs even if they are their "personal" blogs.

Text Messaging and Twitter: Have you ever watched people rapidly texting on their phones? It can be an amazing feat of dexterity and speed. Since phones are pretty small, most messages are either typed with thumbs or one finger. When one uses this unique way of communicating, it is not uncommon for a person to send one hundred or more messages in a day and to have multiple text conversations going on at once. Texting requires a cell phone and a service plan that includes text messages. Text messages use a protocol called Short Message Service (SMS) to send and receive messages as long as 160 characters. If the phone and plan support Multimedia Messaging Service (MMS), the phone can send and receive many media types including long text messages, audio, and video. Most texting is done via short SMS messages.

Of course, texting is not a free online service, but it is closely tied to one called Twitter. Twitter functions as a sort of text-message-driven blog. As such, it has inspired the term "microblogging," given the small space users are allowed for each update. Messages are limited in size to 140 characters, and these small posts are called "tweets." Users have the option to post entries to their Twitter page via cell phone text messages, a program running on their computer, or directly on the Twitter

127

website. The power of Twitter is that a user can choose to "follow" someone on Twitter and that person's messages will show up on the user's Twitter pages as well, or they can be received on the user's phone through a text message. With Twitter you can send a tweet to your Twitter page via a text message, and you can receive tweets from others via text message.

Text messages and especially Twitter messages have a limited number of total characters in a message. Since web addresses you may want to add to a message may be quite long, it may be beneficial to use a URL shortening service like bit.ly or tiny.cc. For example, http://ginghamsburg.org/prayer becomes http://bit.ly/bkgL9O or http://tiny.cc/vqgdv.

You can also use email to send free text messages from a computer or a web application to a cell phone, but unfortunately you need to know the specific cell phone company associated with each cell phone number. All companies set the special email to text message username to the ten-digit cell phone number, but they use different email domains. For example, you can email a text message to a Verizon cell phone number like 123-456-7890 by sending an email to 1234567890@vtext.com for an SMS message or to 1234567890@vzwpix.com for an MMS message. You can find lists of the many email domains for these email-to-text gateways by searching the web for words like *email sms mms gateway*. As we have used this technique, we have found that some of the header information in the email gets included in the text message such as the "from" name and the subject. Since an SMS is only 160 characters long, this can result in truncated messages. As a result, we prefer using MMS messages, which can be quite large. I encourage you to test this approach by sending an email that goes to your own cell phone. You can also cause messages to come to your cell phone by adding your cell phone email address to applications on your website that send emails.

Finally, I would like to point out that we shouldn't send text messages without a recipient's permission because it may be intrusive and it may cost the recipient a fee depending on the person's cell phone plan.

Instant Messaging (IM): IM is a text-based conversation via a web service. Users send short messages to one another that appear only to others in the conversation. IM services often support sending files and audio/video communications as well. IM depends on special servers on the internet that know your username, can tell others your online status, and can enable the IM connection. There are several companies that provide IM servers including America Online (AOL), Microsoft Network (MSN), Google, and Yahoo!. In addition, more comprehensive services like Facebook and MySpace include IM for those who are logged in to their online service. Using IM requires a free individual account on each IM service you use. A special IM application program or a web browser is needed to communicate, and it can run on either a computer or a smart phone. Without additional (free) software, it is only possible to connect to one service at a time using that service's software, so I recommend getting IM software that can support multiple services such as Trillian for PC or Yoono for Mac.

Personally, I dislike typing because I am lousy at it. When I first tried IM, I remember thinking, *I can't believe any human being would like to communicate by typing.* Now, I use it daily and really like it, even though I still dislike typing. IM has a way of growing on you once you get used to it and learn how "IMers" communicate. IM has an interesting lingo with abbreviations to save typing ("lol" = laughing out loud; "brb" = be right back) and special symbols called emoticons that help express emotion:

:-) = smile

;-) = wink

It is not uncommon for IMers to instant message for long periods of time with multiple people, each communicating in a different window. They commonly type characters in all lowercase; all uppercase is considered rude and loud. The etiquette for starting and closing an online exchange over IM is different, too.

IMers may not start with a greeting; instead, they may jump right into a discussion. There may also be long pauses in the discussion as they multitask among other IM sessions and other activities. They may abruptly end the conversation without saying good-bye. They are not being rude; this is just the IM culture.

Audio/Video Communications: Skype is a powerful communications tool that supports text chat, file transfer, audio and video communications, and desktop sharing. We have found that Skype is a powerful tool for team collaboration, especially on our Web-Empowered Church Team. The text chat is useful because it supports group chat and the message size is not limited. Skype is most well known for audio and video communications. The audio enables very clear computer-to-computer communications and audio conferences. Skype users need a Skype account, a microphone and speakers (audio headset is preferred), and reliable high-speed internet. Skype also has paid options for receiving phone calls and calling phones that can possibly save on long-distance charges.

Skype also supports video conferencing. I use video and desktop sharing to conduct remote presentations at various locations around in the world. For example, not long ago I presented to 180 people from the Church of Scotland at an event in Glasgow. With desktop sharing, you can use Skype to show a presentation or to teach someone how to use a program. You can talk to people, and they can see your computer screen on their computer display. When I do presentations to groups at another location (even in other countries), I use a normal computer headset and camera on my computer. On the group's computer, my video appears on a large screen, and my audio is connected to their sound system. It is helpful for me to get feedback as I speak to them if I can see video of the audience from a camera positioned near the large screen and facing the audience. But most critical is the microphone, which allows people to speak to me. It is helpful to use a wireless mic so it can be passed around. It is also helpful if the person speaking can be heard in the room, but its use becomes extremely difficult for me since my voice can provide audio feedback when it is picked up by their microphone and rebroadcast. When this happens, I am forced to turn the audio on my side way down to keep my focus. Remembering to turn off the wireless mic when no one is speaking can help avoid this audio feedback issue.

Office Applications: The technology trend is to move more computer applications from a computer desktop to online. For example, in the past I had to load a tax program on my computer each year and to keep it up-to-date. Now I can do my taxes online. The same is happening with office/administrative applications, and this may be a viable approach to support your organization. In fact, I have learned of several churches that have switched to Google Apps for their mail (Gmail but with your domain in the email address), calendar, documents, spreadsheets, and even presentations. This approach is especially useful when you have virtually no technical staff because there is no application software to install and update, it can be accessed from anywhere, and there is no local backup required. All you need are computers with web browsers and a reliable high-speed internet connection. As I am writing this, Google is offering this service for free to nonprofit organizations. This offer could change, but I see huge potential here and I encourage you to consider this option to web empower some of your administrative activities.

With all online services and especially office applications, there are three major issues to consider. The first and most obvious issue is that your operations become dependent on the reliability of your internet access and the online service. The second and most critical issue is privacy. Christian organizations usually store some information that must be kept private. It is important to review the company security policies so that you feel comfortable that your data will be appropriately protected from compromise. As a result, you may choose to store some data on local computers. Third, as with any storage, there is a small risk that your data could be lost due to some type of failure or even a catastrophe. It is best to create backups of your remote data.

For knowledge and experience related to information technology (IT), I recommend the Church Information Technology RoundTable (CITRT) community at CITRT.org. I was blessed to be a small part of this organization's beginnings. They are passionate about doing IT from a ministry perspective, with excellence for the Kingdom.

A Word of Caution

Scripture reminds us to exercise caution in ministry, and that includes tapping into the great ministry potential of social networking. John 17:15 says that we are to "protect them from the evil one." We need to keep people safe. In 1 Corinthians 8:13, Romans 14:13 and 21, and 1 John 2:10, we are reminded repeatedly not to do things that might tempt our brothers and sisters to stumble. When we go into these online places, we need a strategy that addresses this as both the Great Commission and the need to protect people.

My eyes were opened about this issue after we used a powerful and free video player and streaming server for several years. The company is called RealNetworks and their browser plug-in is called RealPlayer. RealNetworks was a pioneer in web video and enabled us to stream video of our sermons more than a decade ago. In fact, we even did live broadcasts with it. It really was amazing technology and an exciting time for us. To assist our visitors, we added JavaScript on sermon pages that automatically detected if a visitor needed the latest RealPlayer plug-in. If she or he needed it, we provided a convenient link to RealNetworks where the latest version could be downloaded. The user license required that we use only that special page for downloads of their software. This was a bit of a hassle, but most visitors could go to the RealPlayer page and could install the player from the instructions. After that, visitors could watch the streaming video sermons, and life was good for a few years. Then RealNetworks placed a large eye-catching ad on the RealPlayer download page for paid streaming video from a popular pornographic magazine. Then came the calls and the emails to our church. Visitors would say things like "I came to your website to watch a sermon and you directed me to a porn website." Ouch. That hurt. And sadly, our JavaScript was embedded in more than one hundred sermon pages, and we still needed people to download the player in order to watch our sermons. Of course, we scrambled to address the issue and moved away from RealPlayer over time, but this was a good lesson about free services. I think it is important to note that RealNetworks had every legal right to make this change. They invested heavily in the technology and we were using it for free.

In truth, no free online service is truly free. Someone is paying for it, but not necessarily us. Even if investors are funding a hot new online web offering now, at some point they are going to want a return on that investment. One thing that is always consistent about the internet is change. Services that are here and free today may not be so tomorrow. When we choose to use these free online services, it is important to make sure we remain agile enough to discontinue their use or to adapt to the change when that time comes.

Let's look at some less dramatic situations. Social networking websites are extremely popular, and if you are reading this book, you are probably someone who already has an account on at least one social networking website. There are some potential issues with these services that churches and church leaders should watch for.

For example, in conjunction with some of the more involved and mature youth at our church, we went to one of the social networking websites and created a personal webpage for our church's youth ministry. The purposes of the site were to connect with youth, to promote our youth events, and to provide an online daily devotional. We created the personal webpage and quickly had 175 friends, each with links to those friends' personal webpages. That was exciting and encouraging. Then we learned some things that were not so exciting and encouraging. Out of curiosity, we followed the links to each of the 175 friends' pages to see what their personal pages were like. Most were great, even somewhat fun and creative. However, a handful of them included inappropriate (or perhaps illegal) photos with nudity, and some included significant amounts of profanity. Later, we also learned that online sexual predators pursued some students, but thankfully the predators were identified quickly as far as we know.

I have also monitored the ads on social networking websites. In general, they are not a huge issue. At the same time, there are clearly some ads that could "cause a brother or sister to stumble" that range from adult photos to singles-matching websites to promoting online gambling to gimmicks to take your money. Of course, our concern is for people connected to our church who might go to these websites only because our church made that suggestion (promoted it) and then end up in a wrong online place as a result. We would never put these sorts of temptations inside our church or on our main website, so why is it OK to send people to a church-endorsed social networking website with these temptations? There is always a possibility that this may happen when we use these services where we cannot control the content. In addition, from our experiences with the RealNetworks download page, we have learned well that people who visit our website consider links on the website to be endorsements of the website we are linking to. As a result, we are careful about any links we add to outside websites.

All organizations must decide for themselves how to best serve their missions, but my suggestion is to make your main website the primary source of information, so that you are not directing people to social networking sites for essential content. We need to use the popular social websites to connect with the people there, but we also need to work hard to avoid sending people to websites that may not be best for them. As free online services come and go and change, an internet ministry team should set up accounts and post information to these sites, but use the sites as delivery mechanisms to connect to people and to bring people to the main website for more information and safe community. It is also important to monitor all comments posted by visitors and the profile photos of friends in order to keep the online services safer. Comments and photos may need to be removed if they are inappropriate, but more important, they may signal an opportunity to minister to someone in need. As much as possible, any information on the free online service should be conveniently available on the main website as well so there is no need to go elsewhere. We do this in the Web-Empowered Church ministry. We post links to new WEC blog posts on popular social networking websites like Facebook and Twitter, but all the information is posted to the WEC blog on our website. In addition, we are continually looking for ways to add features to our web ministry software to enable organizations using our software to bring features onto their main website to help create both a safe place and a useful one-stop ministry website.

CHAPTER 10

Connecting with People

Using social networking and the online community to connect

What an amazing woman. She is more connected to both God and people than anyone else I know. I am in awe of her passion for living and her confidence that God is in control. She has the kind of faith and wisdom I long for.

Pat was an amazing person. When I told her that, she was somewhat embarrassed and told me I would never want to be like her because she had such evil thoughts. I had to laugh as I imagined the kind of evil thoughts a godly older woman might have. She was a humble servant who was well aware of her sin and totally devoted to the Lord. I listened carefully to anything she said, and I watched how she conducted her life.

Pat loved to write, and she was the right person to form and lead the Internet Ministry Reflection Team—a group of passionate and gifted writers, all unpaid servants, who create daily reflections (devotionals) for our website. Since everyone on the Reflection Team worked from home on their own computers, we set up an online forum to enable them to keep in touch. I was curious to see how this team would work out with so much of the communications dependent on the internet. But I had a feeling it would work out OK.

Pat took charge in her humble yet confident way. She posted to the forum frequently and got the team going quickly. The posts included assignments and lots of encouraging words. Pat clearly had the gift of encouragement. She called the team the "God Pencils" and reminded them that their task as writers was to write down what God was telling them. The team responded with posts that kept a flow of online discussion going. As time went on, I noticed that the online discussions were not only the business of the team; other people would share personal needs and prayer requests, too. For the first time, I saw full prayers posted to a forum. The prayers even ended in "Amen." The group became a close community even though many of them had not met face-to-face. In her quiet but firm way, Pat was like the mom of this online family. She was the strong one who loved everyone, instructed them, and even scolded them at times. This was, and still is today, a very healthy and supportive online community.

When we learned that Pat had lung cancer, roles began to change. Pat shared her difficulties and occasional victories; and the group became the "strong one" who supported and prayed for Pat. Her immune system became so weak that no one could visit her in person, and the telephone was just too intrusive. Posting to the forum was our only method of communication, so we used it to learn how she was doing and to support her.

Throughout this, her strong faith and sense of humor continued to amaze me. She asked for prayer for healing from the sickness and weakness caused by the cancer treatments. She talked about the silver-haired wig she bought to hide her hair loss. When she was at a store wearing her wig, someone complimented her on how beautiful her hair was. She said that she told them "Thank you." She told us that it was not a lie—that it was, in fact, her hair since she had paid for it herself. I laughed until I cried, then prayed for her.

Even when she knew she was very ill, she continued to schedule writing and to lead and encourage the team. Sometimes I would briefly forget she was sick. A few months before her death, she wrote:

> Hi, all you God-fearing Pencils, you! . . . Even though time is marching by fast, I just want to take a minute to thank all of you so very much for your faithfulness to this ministry. . . . What a privilege to be your teammate. . . . As always, looking forward with joyful anticipation as to what your God-messages will be this time. And if the Spirit moves you to send your devotions in early, I will praise His Holy Name and you, too. Take care and may God bless you indeed!

As her body weakened, and she shared her struggles and requested prayer, the posted prayers continued at an increasing rate. "Dear Father in Heaven, we lift our sister Pat into your loving and healing arms." "Father, I lift up Pat to you. I ask for mercies for this warrior of yours." "Thank you, Father, that you have called us to cast every care upon you, because you care. We give our precious Pat to you." "Dear Heavenly Father, we thank you for the warrior you have graced us with in Pat." Pat was showered with prayer and love from the team.

After Pat passed away in November 2002, the team grieved, comforted, and rejoiced together via the online forum. Many writers on the team shared personal stories of how Pat had changed their lives and taught them. I learned I was one of many who looked to her as a model of Christian faith. Her family told me that in her last days, when she could barely get out of bed, she would muster up enough energy to go to her computer to read the posts from the team, but she was too weak to respond. The family said they also printed them and read them to her. She received the prayers and love even when we thought she was not getting them.

Needless to say, we learned a lot from Pat; and I was blessed to know that we were a comfort to her as well even through her last days. And it all happened in online community. In fact, we could not have made these close, personal connections if not for internet technology—the technology some people think of as cold. Since that time, we have seen over and over that internet technology can be a powerful tool to connect with and to minister to people. In many cases, the online community ministers more than the web content we work so hard to produce.

What's Online Community?

Online community happens when online visitors connect in discussion and relationship. Online community is different from most other website features because the visitors provide the content. At the most, the web team provides the rules of the community, the topics, and the mechanism to connect. There are many different web tools that can create opportunities for online community: chat, instant messaging, email lists, forums, social networks, blogs, connectors, wikis, polls, comments, and ratings. Like most tools, each of these has pros and cons in different ministry situations. Previous chapters described the technology tools themselves. This chapter will help you understand the features of each of these tools, where the tools fit in ministry, and challenges you may face as you use them to empower your ministries.

It can be scary allowing visitors to type in whatever they would like to type and then posting it onto a webpage associated with your organization. There are fears of what people might post, of the malicious people this option might attract, and of the online conversation getting out of control. We have included discussion forums on our church website since 1997, and we have added many other community features as well, including online services like Facebook and Twitter. Since then we have had a few minor incidents, but they are minuscule compared with the incredible ministry we have seen. Adding community features is not without risk. By its nature, ministry that connects openly with people can get dirty and risky now and then. However, take precautions to minimize the risks, and the ministry benefit will far outweigh the difficulties. I encourage you to incorporate some form of online community into your internet ministry. The ministry opportunities are worth it.

Ministry with Text Messaging (Texting) and Twitter

Text messages sent to cell phones are ideal for keeping in touch when people may be away from their computers. For example, ministry groups can stay in contact while traveling in multiple vehicles or spread out on a work project. They can also be helpful in mentoring situations such as an adult leader staying in contact with a troubled student. I receive all prayer requests posted to our church website immediately via a text message. While I am traveling, I may get a prayer message and begin praying only seconds after the request is posted.

Twitter opens up even more opportunities for text messages because one text message (tweet) sent to Twitter can result in that message going to many cell phones. This can be used for various kinds of announcements. For example, a team on a mission trip could send tweets about their progress and those back home can follow along. A youth pastor can post thoughts, challenges, and reminders that go straight to students' phones. The message size limits each communication to a brief phrase, but the ability to connect quickly and conveniently wherever people are makes this a powerful ministry tool. Be sure to note the importance of not sending messages too frequently, because they can become annoying or may be ignored.

Ministry with Chat

Chat is one of the older forms of online community, and instant messaging (IM) is a newer form. With chat, visitors connect to an online address referred to as a "chat room" where they "type to talk" to others. As visitors type and submit their messages, everyone currently connected to the chat room immediately sees each new message. Each message is labeled with the username of the visitor who posted it and with the time of the post. A busy chat room can produce a constant flow of messages as each new message is added to the bottom of the list. Chat users need to know the chat server address and the name of the chat room to join in the community, but they do not need to know one another's usernames. For this reason, chat rooms can become great meeting places.

The challenge with using chat in a web ministry is that it must be moderated at all times because problems can occur rapidly and without warning. It is usually best to turn chat rooms on only at specific times and then to turn them off when they are no longer monitored. Moderating may include intervening in the discussion, blocking specific users, or stopping the chat. Chat can be fun and works well for all kinds of live online discussion. For example, you could try a live chat with your pastor or with a visiting Christian music artist before a concert in your area. Churches also use chat as part of interactive online worship experiences. In order to avoid the hassle of requiring special software on each visitor's computer, it is good to host chat on your own website. Look for software that uses Ajax technology. Ajax (Asynchronous JavaScript and XML) allows a web browser to maintain a live connection to the web server, and a live connection enables the chat discussion to dynamically update within the visitors' browsers. This makes it easy for visitors to connect to your live chat room using nothing more than a standard browser. Also, since chat conversations go by so quickly, use chat software that is capable of logging the entire discussion, so that you can go back and review it if necessary.

Ministry with Instant Messenger

IM is similar to chat because IM users also type to talk. IM is unlike chat because connections are directly between people who know each other's IM names, and although more can be added, IM connections are usually between two people. With IM, no connection can take place unless at least one participant knows the username of another participant and initiates a connection. Chat is like a physical room where people can gather in an ad hoc way to discuss a topic, but IM is more like a phone call or a conference call where the participants are specified ahead of time. IM differs from texting because it is used more for online conversations and texting is used more for messages that may require only one response, if any. IM is a popular form of communication. IM fits well at times when a phone call would be a little too intrusive. Also, many smart phones can run an IM program, which adds to the possibilities. IM works great for ministry teams that need to stay in touch, and youth leaders find it to be a popular way to communicate with youth. We use it a lot to communicate among our internet ministry team. When you have a quick question or want to pass along some information, it is amazing how handy it is to send a quick message via IM.

From a youth ministry perspective I absolutely love IM because students are more open to sharing how they are doing and to sharing spiritual things via IM than in person. I instant messaged with a middle school student off and on for over a year when he lost a close friend in a car accident. The student told me how he felt, and we talked about the importance of following Christ now, because life is short. I was glad to be there to support him. Our conversation was probably more open and honest than it might have been if we had been face-to-face. I also instant message with a young girl who has a mischievous streak. She is a smart Christian kid with strong morals and great potential for the future, but I bet parenting her is a challenge. She got in some sort of trouble at school—I never asked the details. She decided to hide it from her parents. I talked to her about the role of parents and the importance of telling her parents when she is having tough times, and she agreed that she should tell her parents. I like that ministering via IM can help youth right where they are right now. Neither of these students lives in my state, yet I was able to support them.

In my experience, youth are more willing to share what they are thinking and feeling inside over IM than they are face-to-face.

They are also more willing to listen to direct talk. IM is a powerful ministry tool. Face-to-face conversation and counseling will always be vital, especially for more serious issues, but IM creates an environment that makes communication a little easier and a little safer; and it enables us to reach youth at different times and over great distances.

Both chat and IM establish community with live text-based communications. The advantage they have over email is that the exchange of messages is immediate and seems more like normal conversation. From a ministry perspective, one issue with any sort of text exchange is that visitors may feel alienated if they type poorly or have a difficult time with writing and spelling. In general this is not an issue since the online culture is usually not too concerned about grammar and spelling. In fact, schoolteachers cringe at the sight of most online messaging. Another issue is that, unlike email or forums, visitors need to communicate at the same point in time. Synchronizing schedules can be difficult, especially if you want to meet online with several people at the same time.

Ministry with Social Networks

Christian community is already a social network so online social networking is a natural fit for us. God invented social networking long before the internet when God created us as social beings with a strong desire to connect and need one another. Social networking helps visitors feel more connected to our organization and to one another. Social networking emphasizes and facilitates an important part of the Christian life—connecting in community. Of course, true community is much more than clicking an "add as friend" link, but it is a first step and it is a connection that we can use to grow a relationship that is deeper and more complete.

Social networking has another huge benefit to Christian pastors and leaders because it enables us to communicate with, to

144

know, to understand, and to serve people more effectively. If a pastor, leader, or organization sets up an account on a social networking website, people will register to become his or her "friend." In this context a "friend" just means that there is a social connection. After that, friends can see each other's pages, comments, photos, and more. For a pastor or leader or just a caring Christian, this connection can be a powerful ministry tool. For example, recently a long-term attendee of our church gave birth to a beautiful baby girl. How do I know this? Facebook. In fact, we learned that she was going to have a baby early and received status updates and photos throughout the pregnancy. We saw photos of "the bump," which is that exciting time when the mother's tummy first started to show that there is a baby inside. We got to see the ultrasound pictures of the developing baby. And toward the end of the pregnancy, we truly laughed out loud (lol) when we saw photos of the mother's older daughter painting a picture on her mother's now-rather-large tummy. Then we saw multiple photos of the newborn baby girl being held by her mother, her father, and her big sister. What a blessing. Throughout the nine months, friends posted encouraging words and prayers, so the family knew that family and friends were watching and caring. In this case, this pregnancy went well and we can rejoice that the mother and baby are doing wonderfully. But if something had gone wrong, we would have known the circumstances and could have jumped in to serve and support this wonderful family. We can debate about whether this sort of openness is a good thing or not, and clearly not everyone shares this openly, and what people share online may not be truthful in all cases, but social networking gives us an additional ministry connection that helps us serve people better.

Earlier I talked about some of the dangers of social networking websites. I encourage you to know those dangers, but then to fully utilize the power of social networking websites to connect with and to know those you serve. Please monitor what people post and check out their photos and other features. You can learn a great deal about people and can probably serve them better both individually and as a congregation. Online social networks are just too valuable to pass up.

Ministry with Email Lists

The first thing most people learn when they get internet access is how to use email, so email is a useful tool for ministry because we can assume that the majority of people will know how to use it. Email, as you can infer from its name, is the electronic version of paper mail. Email lists use standard email, but instead of sending one message to one person, the lists distribute a single email to many different email addresses, similar to how Twitter works with text messages. Software called an "email list server," or a "listserv," can help accomplish this task. This software receives a single email sent to a special list server email address and then replicates and sends that email to all the email addresses included on a subscriber list. The one key feature of mailing lists that differentiates them from many other community tools is that emails are "pushed" out to the subscribers. In other words, the messages come to each subscriber automatically—subscribers don't have to go to a website to get the information. If you need to get a message to a large group of people as quickly as possible, then an email list is a good solution.

Please note that if you set up an email list that supports sending email attachments, it is vital that you also have virus protection on the server to ensure the list does not send out a virus to every subscriber. I have seen this happen, and it does not result in a good feeling. For this reason, and also because attachments can fill visitor email boxes, consider turning off attachments for public email lists.

There are two common configurations for email lists. First, there are lists where a limited number of people are allowed to send email to a group of subscribers. These are ideal for newsletters and announcements. You can also use them for a daily devotional or to send information to a particular group, like all the small-group leaders. This type of list works best when a few people need to get information to a group of people and when you prefer that members of the group not be able to send email to the entire group. The second type of list is one in which any subscriber can send email to all the other subscribers. These can work well to support topical discussions, small groups, and ministry teams. They work best for groups that do not have a lot of discussion because people don't like too many emails, and they work where the discussion does not need to be stored and viewed later.

Our church once had about fifteen or twenty different mailing lists. Some of them grew to several hundred subscribers; and as the community grew, the frequency of emails kept increasing. This was exciting because there was so much interaction. It felt like a really healthy online community. Then, to our surprise, people started unsubscribing in droves. At first we did not know why. Then we learned that when the number of emails reached ten to twenty per day, subscribers felt they were getting too much email, so they unsubscribed. They loved the mailing lists, but could not keep up with all the posts. We offered a digest option that put all emails for one day into one email, but that did not help—it was still too much to read. It was surprising to find that the success of a group ended up driving people away from the group. We tried splitting the group into multiple groups with slightly different topics, but that did not seem to help either. Adding to the difficulty were increasing numbers of new subscribers who often posted questions that previous new subscribers had already asked. The brand-new subscribers had no way of knowing this since they could not see previous posts. We simply had too many posts, and some posts were repeats. More visitors unsubscribed, and the internet team became less popular because of the frustration we created. We learned that we needed a different approach. We ended up moving all our email list groups to a different community tool called forums. Email lists typically work well for smaller groups; we inadvertently used them in a way that did not work well because of the number of emails.

Ministry with Forums

Forums, which are also called "bulletin boards" or "discussion groups," enable visitors to participate in online community on your website. Visitors post messages and read messages that other visitors have posted. Forum links are usually gathered on a main page that lists several forum names and additional information about each forum. Visitors can choose a forum and then read current messages, post new messages, or reply to existing messages. The flow of the conversation from an initial posted message to replies to more replies is often called a "thread."

Forums store all the messages in a database, which is an advantage over email lists because visitors can view previous messages. This helps avoid the email list problem of repeat messages from brand-new subscribers. Storing the messages can also make a forum into an online reference tool. Using the forum search capability, visitors can locate and read through discussions that took place in the past. Our internet ministry team uses a private forum to store information on how to do specific website technical tasks and to announce when we have made software changes. This is how we document what we have learned and what we have done. We can also discuss it online. If there is a need, we can always find the messages later.

Forum software features vary. For example, forums can include message-popularity ratings based on visitor votes, ability to attach a file to a message, ability to display a personal graphic next to each visitor's messages, and ability to send newly posted messages via email. The ability to send emails containing newly posted messages provides some of the benefits of an email list. The main difference between forums with automatic email and email lists is the way visitors post messages. With forums, visitors post messages using a web form on the forum. With email lists, visitors post messages by sending an email to a special email address. Forums give each individual the option of receiving messages via email or via a web browser. Some forums can also report forum activity in RSS feeds. With forums, a visitor can stop receiving messages via email by simply changing a user setting. Unlike email lists, forums have the benefit of archiving previous messages. For most of our online groups, both public and private, we now use a forum that has email capability. Visitors may find forums harder to use than email; however, archival and optional email notifications or RSS make forums an excellent tool for online community.

Ministry with Blogs

A blog, which is short for "web log," is a community tool that enables one person, or sometimes a small group of people, to post a series of messages over time. The blog messages are listed in reverse chronological order with the most recent message at the top of the page. The people posting the messages are called "bloggers," and they are the "owners" of the blog. Blogs, unlike forums, are not usually grouped by subject. So if a website has multiple independent bloggers, there will be a separate blog page for each blogger. Visitors can comment on specific posted messages, but the focus of a blog is on the blogger's messages. In fact, reading the visitors' comments often requires a mouse click to reveal the comments. Like forum entries, blog entries remain stored in a database. Blogs usually have options for finding previous blog messages by date, topic, or keyword search.

Since blogs are usually owned by one person, the messages tend to be informally written and topics are whatever the blogger wants to write about. Some bloggers use blogs as a personal diary. Others tend to blog about one main topic. Some share news. In general, visitors expect bloggers to post frequently. Many bloggers post daily; some post a few times a week. Blogs are useful for informal communications from a leader like a pastor or a youth director. The informal nature of blogs makes them feel more personal and friendly, which makes them a good way to communicate. Plus, they can be fun and are easy to use. If you minister to people who have blogs, it may be helpful to read their blogs to prepare you to serve them better.

Blogging is so popular that its core features appear on other systems like social networking websites and Twitter. The terms may change and the features are often simplified, but at their core they are still a blog and can be applied to ministry in similar ways.

Ministry with Connectors

Connector is a term I use to define a different type of community that we created in the Web-Empowered Church. A connector community is designed to help people who have a need connect with people who can address that need, and to help people who can offer a service connect with people who can use that service. Anyone can publicly post a message containing a need (like a prayer request) or service (like a job opening); however, a reply to a connector message does not get posted publicly like comments on a blog. Instead, the reply is automatically emailed back to the originator, so only the originator of the message receives the reply message. Once the need is fulfilled or the service is used up, the originator removes the posted message. Connector messages are not archived because they are no longer needed once they are fulfilled. The Web-Empowered Church connector can be set to automatically remove messages that are older than a specified number of days and also to filter inappropriate words and links.

Ministry with Wikis

A wiki is a webpage that any visitor or specific group of visitors can edit. This may sound unusual, but with a wiki, visitors can add content to the page, and they can also modify or delete existing content. A wiki is like a big, public whiteboard to which anyone can add in any way and from which anyone can erase anything, although changes can be moderated or undone by an administrator. Visitors use a somewhat unique language to edit the wiki page; however, the language is not difficult to figure out, especially when modifying existing pages. The most famous wiki-based website is probably Wikipedia.org, an online encyclopedia. Wikis work well for collaborative activities such as brainstorming, creating a list, or writing a document. They can also be interesting on a youth website by allowing anyone to add/modify/delete content and pages about some topic. In my personal experience, some visitors are intimidated by having complete ability to modify the page and may not post anything at all. If you try using a wiki, encourage everyone to feel free to participate.

Ministry with Polls

A poll is a multiple-choice question that visitors answer. Most polls are automatically tallied so visitors can see a summary of results as soon as they respond. Polls add interactivity and interest to a website. Polls help build community as visitors get a sense of the way the entire community is responding. We have included a poll question on the front page of the Ginghamsburg website before. The question was designed to get people thinking about the topic of the coming week's sermon. For us, it worked well, but was discontinued because of the time it took us to write the poll question and potential responses each week and the screen space it required.

You can also use polls to gather practical information about visitors. We created a poll question that asked visitors to tell us the speed of their internet connections. You could ask them about Bible version preference or frequency of attendance. Please note that it is impossible to guarantee that visitors do not vote more than once, so while polls can be fun, I recommend that you do not count on their accuracy too heavily.

Comments and Ratings

Comments are opportunities for visitors to type remarks about anything on the current page. Ratings are a way that visitors assign value to the content on a page. These mechanisms provide interactivity and community. For example, a youth website might have a set of pages featuring Christian music artists. Adding comments or a rating system to these pages makes them more popular, interesting, and fun. They are commonly used for blog posts and blog comments as well.

You can also create social-networking links on a page that help a user comment on and share that page with others. The links help the user by constructing the initial message contents and opening a webpage to the selected service like Twitter, Facebook, Blogger, or just email. The user can conveniently edit the message and then post or send it. The website called addthis.com may be a helpful resource if you want to add these links. It provides an HTML code snippet that you can insert on a page to display formatted buttons with links to social networking websites.

Getting Community Started

Many website features can provide some form of online community where people can communicate. Online community happens in an environment that provides healthy social interaction, exchange of opinions, requests and responses, and useful information. Creating and maintaining such an environment require a deliberate effort. One of the most challenging aspects of establishing an online community is keeping it fresh and active. Setting up many different groups is easy, but getting an active discussion going in each group can be a challenge. We've found that a group needs multiple participants posting multiple messages in order to grow, so we start with fewer groups to allow visitors to focus on only those groups.

Once a small set of groups has been created, discussion in each group needs to begin. Most people are reluctant to post messages to a community with few or no messages. Here is one technique that may help get the ball rolling. Gather a small team of people who are interested in supporting a group. Ask the team to begin a discussion and rekindle it as necessary, and to use the community to discuss topics of common interest to most visitors of that group. The purpose is to get the momentum going, build up the number of posted messages, and, one hopes, have a beneficial conversation in the process. Visitors will see the good discussion and join in. Even if they don't join in, many visitors will "listen in" on the discussion and benefit from it without actually posting messages. These visitors are referred to as "lurkers." It is not uncommon for visitors who are suddenly active in the group to claim to have been lurkers for more than a year.

Keeping Healthy

We have found that every online group develops a culture of its own. It is amazing how two groups that are next to each other on the screen will have such different visitors who participate in them. To maintain a healthy culture, assign moderators to each group. ("Group" here means every individual community, no matter what specific community tool is used.) Moderators are responsible for helping maintain a healthy online environment by monitoring every message and ensuring that the messages do not violate the community's rules, which should be posted on the website. Our rules are simple:

1. Please keep your messages short and to topic.
2. Please respect others.
3. No solicitations, please.

To maintain a healthy online culture, the moderator needs to act at the first sign of messages that are rude, crude, or advertise a product or service. Moderators can post responses that help defuse problems before they grow. Moderators can also remove inappropriate messages, but we have found that this can upset the posters. Instead of removing such posts, we edit them to make them less offensive. This approach has the benefit of showing the poster how to write more appropriately and respectfully while allowing the message to remain online. For more serious cases, moderators can contact the individual directly via email and respectfully explain the issue. If treated respectfully, most people will discontinue posting inappropriate messages. In fact, many people will apologize to the group once they realize they have posted inappropriately.

Moderators may occasionally need to send email to visitors who post too often, post off topic, or otherwise disrupt the group. A disruption is identified by comments in visitor messages or complaint emails sent to the moderator. It is best to explain the situation and ask the offenders to post less frequently, thereby giving everyone an opportunity to participate. Most frequent posters do not realize their behavior is offensive, and they adjust their posting accordingly. The moderator is not trying to control the group but to keep the group healthy and safe.

Moderators are also responsible for making sure requests receive responses in a reasonable amount of time, even if they need to do the research themselves. It is frustrating to post a question and not receive a response. We used to assign different monitors to each group, but keeping enough moderators assigned and trained became difficult. Now we use team moderation. Three team members receive all messages from every type of community on the entire website. We hope that at least one member of the team will be available to take action if something needs immediate attention. And that action is often not the task of asking someone to post more appropriately. More frequently, we are alerted of an urgent need, and we need to get help for someone. A moderator who is an active participant in the group will know the visitors in the community better, but our team moderation approach has worked fine, too. As you would expect, the moderator team can get a lot of emails. However, we do not read each message in great detail. Instead, we skim for inflammatory words and solicitations. Reviewing each message usually takes little time.

Difficult Visitors

Membership in online communities is varied, and groups sometimes include difficult visitors. Consider a difficult visitor as a ministry opportunity. It is not logical for someone to come to a church website and be rude to others unless there is some issue with which he or she is struggling. This behavior is probably a cry for help, or at least an indication that the person is hurting. As is often said, hurting people hurt people. We want to help them if we can. At the same time, this type of visitor can damage a healthy online community, and other visitors may choose to leave the community. We need ways to maintain the healthy community while we help the difficult visitor individually. Our experience has been that, with more than three thousand registered users, only two or three difficult people per year disrupt the online community.

In online community that is freely available to the public, it is difficult to totally stop determined and malicious visitors from posting inappropriate messages. Some communities can filter specific words, usually profanity. If you have this option, enable it and consider adding some additional words to the filter list. Another option is to remove a difficult visitor's account. In our experience, this approach causes the visitor to become increasingly angry and does not send the right message when it comes from a church. Churches should not reject anyone because God does not reject anyone. And technically capable visitors can be back online with a new account in very little time. It is seldom wise to delete or modify accounts. Another solution is to change the community setting to moderated, which stops automatic posting of messages. New messages are held from public view until a specified moderator approves them. We try hard to avoid doing this because it reduces the immediacy of the community. Turning on moderation and manually rejecting messages from malicious visitors may tire the visitors so they will quit trying. Of course, using this approach is only for the most difficult cases, which will probably be rare.

The options for connecting with difficult visitors are posting messages to the entire group or directly emailing the difficult visitors. Publicly posting can embarrass them and ordinarily does not help them or the group. Instead, it is usually best to begin with respectful email exchanges, of which the goal is to develop a relationship, understand the purpose of the messages, and ask for their help in respecting the rules of the group. It is also best to encourage direct email exchanges instead of posts to the entire group, which can cause additional disruption. For more difficult challenges, getting these visitors connected with trained people who can help them is important. I call on people from our counseling center when the emotional need seems significant. Then a counselor works with the difficult visitor via email or phone. Through this method, we have been able to help people through some rough times. I have personally exchanged emails with and prayed for difficult visitors for months after an incident. They matter to us and to God.

I strongly suggest that you do not let visitors post on your website without registering for an account that has a verified email address associated with it. If a visitor does not provide a valid email address, there is no way to contact the person directly; and the only option for communication becomes the public community. Verify the email address by having the registration software send an email containing a randomly generated link to the website. When the visitor receives the email and clicks the link, the email address is automatically verified and the new account is enabled. This approach ensures that each email address is valid. To re-verify email addresses, send an email to everyone with an account, then remove accounts for email addresses that are rejected (bounce). We try to verify email addresses yearly.

One of our biggest challenges has been avoiding messages that are focused more on selling something than on the group topic or community. These are a form of spam—undesired and intrusive advertising—but they are not always blatant spam and can be disruptive to a group. An example is a web developer who constantly refers to her ability to help (for a fee) visitors in the group. It seems as though the purpose of her involvement is solely to divert the discussion and attract new attention to her business. Some people are less subtle and post typical spam messages. As spammers have told us, the attraction to spammers is that a given group provides easy access to a targeted audience of potential customers—new business is just one post away. For example, we have a motorcycle ministry that has its own forum. If a visitor has a business that customizes motorcycles, he or she may be tempted to advertise on the forum. We don't mind occasional discussion about a business or product, but we do mind when messages feel like commercials.

We usually use the same techniques with spammers that we use with other difficult visitors. We email them directly and ask them not to post advertisements. In a few cases this has not worked. As a last resort to address the problem, we post a message to the entire group. We inform the group of our efforts to stop the spammer's messages via repeated private email exchanges. We tell the group that the spammer has continued to defy the group rules. We then ask the group to collectively agree to boycott the spammer's product or service. Members of the group are usually quick to post messages supporting the boycott. So far, this technique has worked well, and the spammers have immediately discontinued posting messages.

How Community Works

We have learned a lot about how communities work as we have experienced hosting online community over the years at Ginghamsburg Church. This may sound obvious, but one thing we have learned is that online community is a whole lot like face-to-face community. Visitors are people communicating via a different mechanism, but they are still people. What follow are a few of the issues we have noticed over the years. We have not conducted scientific, psychological analysis; these are merely observations and experiences that might be helpful to you.

Intimidation: We have been surprised at how many visitors are reluctant to post a message to a group. Some say they are unsure about the technology or don't want to show their ignorance. Others seem to be concerned that the group will respond negatively to a posted message. In the beginning, most people are intimidated by the technology, and this keeps them from posting messages even when they would like to. The result is many lurkers. We estimate that about 90 percent of visitors are lurkers—those who read but do not post messages. At the same time, we've found that once visitors begin posting messages, much of their fear goes away, and we generally see more messages from them in the future.

Anonymity: By its nature, posting messages to a community is more anonymous than many other types of conversation. As a result, once visitors overcome the intimidation of the technology and of posting a message, they are likely to share personal stories. The anonymous feeling of online community allows visitors to express themselves more freely. Online community can also break down barriers for those who are of different races, shy or uncomfortable around people, or self-conscious about their appearance. From a ministry perspective, the anonymity may allow us to have more open and frank discussions, and to help people with various life issues. We also need to keep an eye out for visitors who are not who they claim to be. This problem is partially alleviated by the requirement to register with a valid email address. Visitors know that we can contact them if needed. So far, the challenge of visitors pretending to be someone they are not has not been a problem for us.

Group Environment: We have learned that each group takes on a unique environment defined by the visitors who post most of the messages. Groups vary in the formality of the discussion, acceptance of differing opinions and debate, acceptance of new visitors ("newbies"), desire to help others, and sense of community. Visitors will not stay in the group if they don't like the environment. Some of our groups have gotten into strong debates that lead to angry messages and personal attacks. This can quickly have an impact upon the health of the group, so it is important for the moderator to address these issues quickly and make sure the situation is resolved.

Peer Pressure: We did not anticipate the significance of peer pressure. Peer pressure is often what keeps the group healthy. We consider a group healthy if the group can police itself. One example of this behavior is when someone makes a rude comment, and one or two others post messages that let the originator of the comment know that his or her behavior is unacceptable. Comments like "Hey, no need to get nasty" or "Please cut the person some slack" are signs of positive peer pressure in action. We find that occasional peer pressure is a useful tool to help guide the group. Because peer pressure keeps people accountable, there are probably fewer problems with online community than most churches anticipate.

Relationships: We have seen online community facilitate close relationships. We have groups where most visitors have never met one another, yet many members consider other group members to be their close friends. They know about one another's family and jobs, and talk about all sorts of issues. We had one group decide to get together for a live pizza party. It was fascinating to see how close people could be who had not met face-to-face. The group was like a family and had a great time together. They still continue the relationship online.

Team Collaboration: One power of online community is facilitating team collaboration. We have multiple teams that only occasionally meet in person, yet they are in frequent conversation online via collaborative community. We use private forums to make announcements, task team members, discuss plans, request assistance, get to know people, and more. The forums allow team members to participate when time permits and from any location. The forum also keeps all team members in the loop so everyone knows what is happening within the team. The result is team members who are informed and feel like they are part of the team without the need for frequent meetings. This is especially true of our Reflection and Internet Ministry teams.

Technical Support: Web ministries commonly get requests for assistance with activities such as registering for an account, resetting a password, subscribing to receive messages via email, changing an email address, and removing an account. Visitors can do all these things via available pages, but many of them find it to difficult or are unwilling to learn. We used to email instructions on how to perform the functions, but this confused them more and often resulted in more email exchanges and increased frustration for all. Now we make the changes and return an email to say that the requested change was made. Visitors appear to be satisfied with this approach, and we have found that the technical support team spends less time making the changes than it used to spend describing how to make the changes.

A Good Thing

Community-based web tools are valuable additions to a web ministry. Even though the effort to initiate and maintain online community can be significant, the ministry benefits can be much greater. We have received numerous emails from visitors all over the world who thanked us for our community features. We also find that teams can develop more synergy when they use online community to stay in touch. Community-based web tools connect people to people and allow them to work and learn together. Visitors can participate whenever they have time and from wherever they are located. Online community works especially well for congregations because a church is by definition a community.

CHAPTER 11

Teaching and Discipleship

Training and equipping the body of Christ

In John 13:13-15, Jesus says, "You call me Teacher and Lord—and you are right, for that is what I am. So if I, your Lord and Teacher, have washed your feet, you also ought to wash one another's feet. For I have set you an example, that you also should do as I have done to you."

Besides being our Lord and Savior, Jesus was the greatest mentor and teacher of all time. He taught by demonstrating how life should be lived and through stories and instruction. Jesus directed us to do as he did—to mentor and to teach. The internet offers some wonderful opportunities for online instruction of all types. In addition to more traditional "book learning" where students read several pages and then take a test, the internet allows us to include photo, audio, video, and interactivity. Now teaching can become less rigid and more self-guided where the students research and learn according to their own desires and interests. We can connect students with their teachers in a variety of different ways including chat, audio conferences, forums, and live video. And we can create peer-learning opportunities that connect groups of students and teachers to learn from each other. Much of the day-to-day work of the church is teaching in one form or another, and the internet offers great opportunities for us to expand our ability to train and equip the body of Christ to be what Jesus taught us to be.

Classroom-Like Teaching

One of the challenges at most churches is finding enough teachers, especially for classes that are more about study than fellowship. A creative solution is to offer classes online. Traditional classes where the teacher does most of the talking or classes that can be partitioned into noninteractive components are good choices for online classes. There are several online teaching systems that allow you to create classes. In our experience, most teachers prefer not to create online classes. They simply want to teach. An approach that many teachers prefer is to record the teaching sessions in either audio or video format during each class. The online class works best if the teacher uses charts, which are commonly created in PowerPoint. The web team can combine the audio or video with the charts to create an online class.

When the Web-Empowered Church Team (WEC) first started trying this approach, I expected it to be very popular and for churches to begin posting classes this way. Yet a significant challenge to online teaching is keeping the classes copyright free, a necessity if classes are posted publicly on the internet. For example, live classes often work through a copyrighted book, or teachers use copyrighted material to supplement their class. For online classes, either class material needs to be original, or you need to obtain permission from the publisher to allow copyrighted content online.

Another way to potentially address copyright issues is to control online access to the class and, for the purpose of copyright conformance, treat online classes exactly as you treat live classes. You need to count attendees and obey any copyright rules that would apply to a physical classroom. This is generally acceptable in school settings, but you should check with the publisher or seek legal advice to be sure.

WEC has a ministry extension that allows you to create a presentation, such as a class, that uses audio or video with charts that change automatically during the presentation. While watching the class, a visitor can move forward and backward in the presentation, and the charts and video will follow along. To create the class, you must create the audio or video files and match the charts to image files. By using these files and noting the designated times for the charts to change, the extension delivers an online presentation of a class on your website. You can create multiple online classes simply by recording teachers who are teaching each class, generating the necessary files, and using this extension. In our experience, it will take about three times as long to create an online class as was the duration of the class that was recorded, so long as minimal video editing is needed. For example, a one-hour recorded class takes approximately three hours to create, and most of that time is spent capturing, editing, rendering, and uploading the video.

There are several different models for online classes that are worth trying:

1. Classes are totally online and include an online forum that allows attendees and the instructor to discuss the current class content. Extra class materials are also posted to the web. By using this method a teacher can support several classes at one time. You can arrange to have classes on a flexible schedule that allows students to take them at any time or pace, or you can set classes on a specific schedule.
2. The main content of the class is provided online, and the class meets in person on a periodic basis for interactive discussion about the current topic.
3. The class is offered live, but attendees have the option of attending either the online class or the live class. The online class is also an excellent way to catch up if an attendee misses a class.

In support of either online or live classes, the website can list available courses with course descriptions, provide online course sign-up, help people track which courses they have taken, and provide a way to order resources such as books. For any online class, you could hold discussion through a forum, email list, or chat. In addition, you could add online quizzes to test participants' understanding.

Teaching younger children via the web can be more difficult because they may not be able to read, or they may not know how to operate a computer very well. If you have skills in programming in Flash, you can create games that teach Bible stories and concepts, as even preschoolers can use a mouse to click pictures or otherwise respond to audio cues. The most effective use of the web for teaching children is equipping parents or guardians to teach their children. You can use the web to supply all kinds of teaching resources to augment what the children learn at church. In addition, parents may find an online forum helpful for discussing various parenting challenges.

Group Learning

Another way to disciple people is through an online Bible study. These are fairly common among churches, and some youth groups use them. Churches usually set up an online Bible study with an e-mail list or a forum to allow the group to communicate. The leader of the study periodically posts Scripture references and questions. Participants read the Scriptures and respond to the questions online. The group discusses the topic and the answers. Another mechanism for group learning is a wiki or shared Google document that a group can work on together to write about a designated topic. These approaches result in both independent and peer learning, and can result in additional insights that would not be possible by learning in more traditional ways.

Daily Devotionals

A devotional is a short writing or Bible verse that helps visitors focus on God on a regular basis. Daily devotionals are difficult to include in your web ministry because they require fresh content every day. If you can keep up with the content generation, daily devotionals can be a powerful tool for personal growth for both adults and youth within your church. In order to share the load, multiple staff can generate the content and possibly enlist an unpaid servant team. One way to get started and to simplify devotional content generation is to provide only a daily Scripture reference. Selecting Scripture references from a current course of study or from the sermon simplifies the selection process while reinforcing the current teaching. To encourage daily participation, offer the daily devotional via email. The individual devotionals are entered well ahead of time, and the devotional for the current day is automatically emailed to subscribers the night before—usually shortly after midnight to ensure that it is available to those who wake up early. You can also provide the devotional on paper for people who do not have internet access.

WEC has a software extension that adds more features to a devotional. It generates a devotional page to which visitors go daily. The page changes automatically each day, and a visitor can navigate to previous or future days' pages. You can organize the content into multiple categories and set the content duration for any amount of time. For example, if you are studying biblical topics, name one category "topic" and include a summary of the current topic. Set this content to remain for several days, or even weeks, while content in other categories changes daily.

The extension also supports a personal journal where a visitor who is logged on can enter his or her own notes or thoughts. Visitors use the personal journal editor to enter and then nicely format their notes by setting text attributes like bold, italics, and color. Journal information is kept private. Visitors see only their own journal entries, and the entries are encrypted in the database for additional protection.

You can use the WEC discussion extension along with the devotional to add community discussion and group learning. This enables the community to ask questions and share personal insights related to the current devotional. We find that this feature provides additional incentive to come to the devotional page because visitors want to monitor the latest posts to the online discussion.

Interactive Self-Learning

Recently we partnered with MaxPoint Ministries to create a unique interactive learning environment called 24-7 Discipleship. It begins with a spiritual self-assessment that helps place the user in one of five stages of spiritual development. The assessment uses a WEC extension we developed in partnership with The United Methodist Church of the Resurrection in Leawood, Kansas. The extension helps people identify their spiritual gifts or the next steps to take in their spiritual growth. Users can then begin working through the appropriate course. Each day they view a short video teaching, a Scripture reading, a prayer, a quotation, an action step, and an opportunity to write in a personal journal. The software remembers how far users have progressed and makes it impossible for them to move to the next lesson until the next day. This keeps users from rushing through the lessons and gives them time to think about what they have learned. Each learning experience lasts thirty days. I really like this system of learning because it is personalized and experiential due to all of the different elements. The website also includes additional Bible studies for individuals or groups, the ability to post prayer requests, and administrative features to track the progress of all the users. You can learn more about the 24-7 Discipleship at http://mymaxpoint.com. You can also get a customized version for your organization through MaxPoint at http://maxpoint.org. This is a powerful learning tool, and the extensions used to create it are available from WEC.

Sermons

Sermons are usually the most valuable content a church has to offer on the web. A great deal of effort goes into them, their content is usually original (or at least is not copyrighted by an outside source), and most churches produce them every week. You can produce sermons in multiple formats including text, audio, and video, and can deliver them as webpages, PDF files, RSS, and podcasts. In our experience, the text version is most popular. Adding sermon text to a website is fairly easy if your pastor writes out sermons in detail, but more difficult if you need to transcribe them from audio recordings. Text also offers the huge advantage of being searchable—both on your website and across the internet. If you provide a text sermon, make it a printable version because people often print sermons to read or give to others. If you use PDF to make a printable version, create webpages containing the sermon text for online viewing and to make the text more searchable. Since an oral sermon translated verbatim can be choppy and unorganized, consider editing sermons to ensure they work well as written information. You may need to insert section titles and break blocks of text into paragraphs in order to help make the sermon more readable.

Audio and video also offer a chance to expand the audience because individual visitors generally have a preference for one particular format. For example, some people would never stop what they're doing to read all the text from a sermon, but they would listen to sermon audio on an MP3 player, perhaps even offline while they drive or exercise. RSS feeds that link to your text sermons or podcast for audio or video sermons expand the audience to include people who prefer a certain method of delivery. Adding formats provides the platform for a larger audience.

You can also augment the sermon with additional features, such as a group or individual Bible study that references many of the same Scriptures. You could also include a poll question or even a survey to get people thinking about the sermon topic. Some churches include the bulletin with the other sermon resources because it includes the sermon outline and other related information. You can also develop an online community to encourage open discussion about the sermon topic. If the pastor is willing to participate in the discussion, the community could be even more popular and fruitful.

At Ginghamsburg Church we often synchronize the topics and Scriptures in our daily devotional and personal and group Bible studies with the sermon topic.

WEC has a sermon extension that supports these features and also archives sermon data, such as notes and PowerPoint files, that will not be made available publicly but fit well with the other sermon information. The result is a useful place to store all the sermon resources for later retrieval by those who have authorized access. The sermon extension supports many different resources that you name and define. It will list resources, search for them, display them, and can podcast. WEC also has an extension that can play audio MP3 files and one that can play Flash video.

Online Worship Experience

Online worship includes the sermons but attempts to create a more complete worship experience. The biggest technology challenge is to make the visitor feel like he or she is in corporate worship with others. Online worship needs video and audio in order to make it an experience. Key is the inclusion of music and other elements found in a common worship experience. The events are scheduled at specific times in order to allow people to gather to worship together, and to address copyright limitations by treating the event like a physical event with a known number of attendees. An event can be streamed live, a mix of live and prerecorded events, or purely recorded. As I have talked with several churches that offer online worship, most see little advantage in live online worship for many of the same reasons live television is less common now. It is more costly to provide live experiences because additional equipment and redundancy are required to ensure reliable and quality delivery week after week. But perhaps more important, live online events are limited to specific days and specific times when physical events are happening. For example, if we live broadcast our main worship celebration starting at 10:15 a.m. in Ohio, someone in California would need to be online at 7:15 a.m. in order to watch it. If it is recorded, we have the option of offering online worship at various convenient days and times to reach many more people. In addition, if the event is prerecorded, it can be edited to improve quality. For example, you may want to keep an offering time, but waiting the full duration as the offering plates are physically passed around the room may not work well for someone watching online who could choose to give an offering very quickly electronically. Life Church in Oklahoma (see LifeChurch.tv and ChurchOnline.org) is an example of a church that maximizes the capabilities of what they call "Church Online." Life Church offers more than twenty weekly "Church Online" worship experiences on various weekdays and times. These events are prerecorded and edited for the online worship experience including additional video segments from a "Church Online" pastor. Life Church and most churches rely on a sermon management system to allow access to all previously recorded sermons, but an online worship experience is only offered for one week. A church could consistently offer the current week's sermon or a previous week's sermon if more time is needed for editing and other preparation.

Many churches treat and refer to online worship as just another church site or venue along with other physical sites. They may even have an official online site pastor. Choosing days and times for online worship is done similar to the way they are chosen for a physical site. In fact, online ministry of all types almost always parallels what we do in person because we are still ministering to people, just using a different communications mechanism. Times are chosen based on when people would want to join in and when it is practical to schedule online worship leaders (if you use them). As with a physical worship event, fewer options are better if it is difficult to get a group of people watching together. An online worship leader is responsible for facilitating and monitoring any activity that allows people to interact in online worship, including monitoring their posts. If people cannot post in a live chat or similar system, the event loses some of the live and interactive feel of worshiping together and participating.

Video production has a few differences from physical events. Speakers should never refer to the current time as "tonight" or "this morning" because someone could be watching at any time and such a reference would disrupt the live feel. There is also great value in looking into the camera more and especially welcoming everyone, including those watching online. Making these adjustments makes the experience feel more personal to online visitors instead of making visitors feel they are only casual observers watching someone speaking to others. Some churches have the online pastor speak to the online community before and after the sermon. The online worship event can include announcements if they make sense for the online audience, or the event may include custom announcements just for the online community. As I mentioned previously, the worship event includes music and the sermon. An offering and an attendance registration opportunity are additional options.

Here are some possible features you could include in online worship:

1. Users can preregister for an event reminder via email or text message that will contain the event date and time,

sermon title and speaker, and a link to the online worship page. Users will choose a worship day/time to be notified. A message could say, "In 30 minutes, online worship will begin with Pastor Joe speaking on Relationships. See http://ourchurch.org/worship."

2. A countdown timer can display the days, hours, minutes, and seconds until the next online event.

3. It is important to encourage people to register for a website account and to log in. An account provides additional tracking information, but more important, it gives visitors access to additional web ministry features. It is also best to offer an alternative to worship without the account for those who would be pushed away by the account requirement.

4. A form could be available to record attendance. If the person is registered and logged in to her or his website account, the attendance process should be automatic or at least simplified. The form needs to support more than one person if multiple people are watching from one computer.

5. Visitors can register for next week's reminder email/text message by simply choosing an option on the attendance registration form.

6. Worship video and features can be viewed or used online on a computer or via a smart phone. Cell phones may require downloading an extra application to support online worship.

7. People who have a website account and login can take personal notes that are saved and stored with the archived sermons. The notes can also be automatically sent to an email address at the end of the event without the need for a website account.

8. People can take notes in a simplified rich text editor with the option of having the sermon outline pre-entered.

9. A section of the browser window can display the slides from the sermon or other special announcements for the online audience. It could also have links that pertain to the current sermon discussion, and the attendance or electronic giving form can display there at the appropriate times.

10. It can be helpful to show a progress bar indicating how far the service has progressed.

11. Live chat is a great community-building tool for online attendees, but should be facilitated and moderated by a leader whose chat messages are distinguishable from other chat participants. Giving moderators the ability to ban users and to filter bad language is a must. Giving participants the ability to chat privately with the leader could be helpful for people with additional private needs or fear of posting publicly.

12. As the total number of online worshipers grows, it can be valuable to display the number and location (city) of worshipers. The location could be displayed on a map. But if the total number is too few, then it is best not to provide this information. The goal is to enhance the community feel.

13. The overall appearance of some visual elements on the online worship page could change based on the sermon topic or a sermon series.

14. The online worship page can include other helpful but fixed links that direct people to post prayer requests, register for an event, get additional help, buy a CD, get technical help if the online worship page is not operating correctly, and so on.

15. You could also include participatory features such as the ability to light a virtual candle, post prayer requests, or indicate that you are raising your hands in praise.

Live Webinars and Meetings

Live webinars (web seminars) and meetings are useful for mentoring or teaching activities, fostering bidirectional interaction between speakers and attendees. Depending on your requirements, you have a few options.

1. You can use a format similar to online worship where visitors communicate via chat to ask questions. However, the speaker can monitor chat more closely and can answer questions or comment based on those live chat entries.
2. A tool like Skype, as I mentioned before, can provide some communication features as well, especially for remote presentations to a group at another location or to a small group.
3. There are also systems that are designed for online collaboration, meetings, or webinars. These systems often include features like desktop sharing, a whiteboard, co-browsing of websites, and video or audio conferencing. Some can also record and play back the event. DimDim is one example of an open-source tool that can support live meetings and webinars. See http://dimdim.com.

Mentoring

Given the rising age of clergy in many denominations, there seems to be a growing desire among senior pastors to mentor younger up-and-coming pastors. Online mentoring enables more experienced people to leave a legacy and to help ensure the viability of future generations. We created an online mentoring system for the Young Clergy Network founded by Pastor Adam Hamilton of The United Methodist Church of the Resurrection in Leawood, Kansas, and Pastor Michael Slaughter of Ginghamsburg Church in Tipp City, Ohio. A committed group of younger pastors (chosen through application) participate in regular online activities as well as multiple in-person events. Since this was a new concept, we tried many different features available in the WEC. The website is private and requires a username and password in order to access it. The features include member photos and personal information, prayer requests, a discussion forum, private live chat, daily devotions, mentors' blogs, and assignments. Of course, the power of a mentoring system like this is the opportunity for younger pastors to get advice and learn in a private and safe environment where they have direct access to mentors. Even a simple forum could serve this purpose and make a huge difference in the future of the church.

CHAPTER 12

Empowering Ministries

Many ways you can web empower your ministries

It's a web-empowered church. Online care, service, administration, communications, and more.

A sixteen-year-old student gets a text message that the youth leader updated his blog. He goes to his computer to check out the youth leader's blog post where he learns there is a mission trip coming up. He sees that the youth leader is online, so he contacts the youth leader via instant messenger to ask about the mission trip. The youth leader tells him more about the trip and sends him a link to a webpage containing all the trip details. He suggests that the student check out the video, photo slideshow, and the recorded daily Twitter feed from last year's trip. The youth leader asks how the student has been doing and says he looks forward to seeing the student at youth group this week. The student gets on the online youth forums and posts a question asking if anyone else is going on the trip because it sounds really cool. He then sends his parents an email with a link to a page that provides all the details about the trip, the costs, and a form that allows them to sign up and pay for the trip online.

A single parent wakes up before her children, and before the chaos of the day starts. She goes online to do her daily devotion and journaling. She is really touched by the day's Scripture reading, so she writes in her private online journal and then decides to post her thoughts to the public discussion group where she can share with others who are following along in the same devotional. She attends church each week and likes to pray for others, so she chooses to receive all church prayer requests via both email and text message using the online prayer system. She carefully reads through the requests and prays for each of them. Next, she goes to the single-parent forum and reads through the latest posts from other Christian single parents. Online they talk about the challenges of single parenting, pray for one another, and plan events that they do together as a group. When times are difficult, the single-parent forum helps her keep it all together. She has quickly accessible friends who understand the challenges of single parenting.

A businessperson travels and works a lot of hours, including frequent trips on the weekends. There are few chances for him to participate at church events, but he does so whenever he can. While traveling he uses either his laptop or his smart phone to connect to the church website where he watches the sermons every week via video. He is also taking an online class at the church. The teaching is available via video, and he can download the written class resources and assignments. The class includes an online discussion area where he posts questions that the teacher and others taking the class respond to. He is also in a private online men's accountability group where a handful of brothers in Christ share openly and keep one another accountable. They get together in person whenever they can, but their busy schedules make an online group a good way to keep connected.

A woman who lives thousands of miles away from your church is seeking to learn about Jesus. She is not a Christian and is looking for safe ways to privately learn about the Christian faith. She searches the internet with various search words of interest, just happens to find a particular sermon on your church website, and reads it. She browses the rest of the website and reads about what your church believes. She also reads through the spiritual discussions on your online forums. She sees pictures of people having fun together, worshiping, and serving. She gets a sense of what it is to be a Christian and to be in a healthy church community. She may never post to your website or contact you in any way. She may only show up as a number on the website statistics page. Yet you are part of a process that ultimately leads her to Christ.

Web Empowering Your Ministries

As the stories above indicate, a fully web-empowered church is able to minister 24/7 to anyone with internet access via computer or cell phone. The empowerment comes from combining the features of a variety of internet tools to more effectively deliver content that churches already have, enhance church administrative functions, and connect people in community.

Don't be troubled about getting all the many available features on your website. Creating an excellent internet ministry involves persistence over time. Do your best to add appropriate features to your website as you are able and ready. Not every feature will fit your ministry or those you serve. As you continue to add features and content, your church will become increasingly web empowered in its own way. You don't need to feel pressured— in fact, there is value in adding features slowly so that your organization and visitors can learn the new features and grow along with your web ministry. With the help of the Web-Empowered Church (WEC) software, you can quickly install features that took years to develop and refine.

The previous two chapters focused on web-empowering community and teaching. This chapter describes additional ways you can empower your ministries. The creative challenge comes from mixing, matching, and using the web tools I've listed in real ministry situations. This chapter contains different internet ministry ideas, most of which have been tried and tested in real ministry situations. This chapter will also introduce you to several WEC ministry extensions and other TYPO3 extensions that can be used in ministry. You can use these ideas exactly as they are or use them to trigger new and better ideas.

Prayer

Prayer is an important part of any Christian ministry. Many churches track prayer requests and also have a group of people who pray specifically for the requests. A common way to gather prayer requests on a website is to use an email form. An email form is a webpage containing form fields that visitors fill out. When visitors complete the form, they submit it, and the contents of the form are automatically emailed to one or more designated email addresses. Email forms are not completely secure—a person with the knowledge and network access could theoretically intercept the information. Interception is unlikely, but if you require a high level of confidentiality, you may not want to use web forms, or you may want to encrypt the data in some way. At most churches, the web alone will not meet all needs for requesting prayer, so provide a phone number people can call to request prayer.

For less personal requests, you can use a community prayer system. WEC provides one that uses a connector community. The advantage of community prayer is that people can share needs quickly and publicly, and the community can come together to support them and pray for their requests. In our experience, many people like to participate in this way. Our church gets more prayer posts than any other type of post to its website. The most posted to page on the website is a slight variation of our main prayer request page—the e-candle page. Visitors post a thought or prayer and light a virtual candle created with an animated GIF. Every posted message includes a candle, and all the candles flicker together. There have been thousands of e-candle messages posted by people from around the world. Many of the messages are quite serious, related to loved ones who have passed away or are seriously ill, wars and soldiers, salvation of loved ones, and marriage problems. This page's dark colors and flickering candles convey a sense of reverence.

The WEC software extension generates an online prayer request page where visitors can publicly post prayer requests. The most recent requests are listed at the top of the page. You can configure the extension to allow all visitors or only visitors with accounts to post requests. Visitors have the option of posting anonymously or by name. (The requests are all posted publicly, but anonymous requests do not include the name of the requester.) Once a request is posted, the requester has the option of allowing responses, so that anyone viewing the request can send the requester a personal note. The note is entered on a web form and automatically sent to the original poster via email, so requesters who posted anonymously can receive personal notes while remaining anonymous. The WEC software extension also supports sending the contents of all new prayer requests via email when they are posted, and this can be sent via email or text message. Visitors subscribe to receive prayer requests via email, and prayer team members use this feature in order to provide immediate prayer support. The extension also supports other administrative features such as automatically filtering inappropriate language, automatically deleting the oldest prayer requests after a specified time, and optionally requiring that a moderator review the request before it is posted publicly on the website.

A web-empowered church in Colorado using this prayer feature contacted us by phone. The pastor told us that a young woman involved in a gang witnessed her boyfriend's murder in a gang fight. In desperation, she posted a message to his church's prayer page even though that church did not know her. That prayer request eventually enabled her to get counseling from that church and she came to know Jesus Christ. Since that time, she has been physically beaten for her faith and for leaving the gang, but she has also been used by God to help grow a gang ministry that is showing gang members a better way. As a result, other gang members are leaving gangs and coming to Christ. Stories like this remind us of the importance of internet ministry. Through this prayer feature, we also continue to see people in the community praying for, comforting, and supporting visitors who share prayer requests online. This is community, and these connections would not have happened if not for online community prayer.

Service

Encouraging service and connecting people to unpaid servant (volunteer) positions in an organization can be challenging. People who want to get involved are not always sure what the needs and opportunities are. You can help by including on the website a list describing the opportunities to serve and an email form visitors can use to request more information or to sign up to begin serving. You can also use the website to help keep track of where people are serving.

WEC has a software extension that automates much of this process and provides many powerful features to encourage serving. Leaders in the church enter servant opportunities, and each entry includes fields for the name of the opportunity, the name of the ministry, a description of the opportunity, the location of where the service will occur, the dates and times of service, any required qualifications or training, and the point of contact. Leaders can also cross-list each opportunity with any number of skills, interests, spiritual gifts, and strengths from a list configured according to a ministry's needs. Once a leader enters an opportunity into the list database, it immediately becomes available on the website. Visitors can browse through the list of opportunities or search for opportunities based on their personal skills. For example, if a visitor selects "computers," most of the opportunities in the internet ministry will show up on the resulting list. Visitors can narrow the search by selecting multiple skills and searching for opportunities that match all the skills. Once visitors identify interesting opportunities, they can print out a list, or they can commit to the opportunity by submitting a web form. When a visitor submits the form, an email containing all the information is sent to the service opportunity contact person and, optionally, to an administrator.

At Ginghamsburg, we have used this capability for several years to match hundreds of people to servant opportunities. This tool is also used for our member class and by our ministry leaders who help people find opportunities to serve.

North Coast Church is a large web-empowered church in Vista, California, that has taken weekend community service to a whole new level. Every so often, the church conducts its Weekend of Service with the slogan "the church has left the building." They promote and coordinate this huge event using their WEC-based website. They post fun and challenging videos on their website to encourage participation, communicate the specific project needs and receive donations of needed supplies and equipment, recruit and instruct many project leaders, receive prayer requests, manage the servant sign-up, and schedule the serving opportunities. And they report the amazing results. On their most recent Weekend of Service they closed the church and went out to work throughout the community. More than five thousand volunteers participated in more than one hundred different community projects. They used more than nine hundred gallons of paint, one thousand pieces of lumber, and one hundred eighty dumpsters. The estimated value of the work exceeded $1 million. The excitement attracted news media coverage, but most important, the community saw the church in action. And now, with the help of the North Coast web ministry, other churches have been using WEC-based websites to provide the online support for their own weekends of service.

Evangelism

As Christians, we are called to offer Christ to those who do not know him. The web provides many ways to creatively and effectively communicate this message through words, graphics, animation, sound, and video. Every church website should include the message of salvation, even if it is only in an "about us" section describing what the church believes. Some churches choose a "questions and answers" (Q & A) format to address specific questions visitors may have about the church, salvation, or the Bible. If you want to include more entries than fit comfortably on a single webpage, then a searchable "knowledge base" database may be helpful. Each entry in the knowledge base has a title (the question) and information (the answer to the question). WEC has a knowledge base extension that enables visitors to search for entries containing specific keywords or to browse entries by category. Visitors can see a list of all the categories, a list of the most recent entries, and a list of most frequently viewed entries.

Bringing people to your website for the purpose of evangelism is a challenge. One way to help people find your website is to include content that search engines will index. I hope that churches around the world will flood the internet with meaningful content on their websites so that when visitors use a search engine to search for keywords or phrases, the results list will almost always include churches. At Ginghamsburg, visitors from other religions have sent us email saying they found a sermon on our website by typing in a phrase. In two cases, the sermons were about other religions, and the visitors had questions and comments about what the sermon said about their religions. We had an opportunity to share why and how we follow Jesus.

Another less common but effective way to attract non-Christians to your website is to advertise on non-Christian websites. For example, you could purchase specific Google AdWords that provide a link to your website based on specific words visitors enter. This may be a viable approach for websites focused on evangelism.

As mentioned in chapter 9, the internet—specifically free online services that promote social networking—is a powerful mission field for evangelism. I encourage you to deliberately and methodically send missionaries and mission teams out to places where they can connect with people on the internet to be "salt and light" in the world. Be careful to prepare people for this mission field, and send only mature Christians who can manage the various pressures and temptations. If churches around the world jump into the dirty and unhealthy online places such as chat rooms and forums about off-color topics, the internet will become a much safer place, people in great need will be helped, people will be introduced to Christ, and lives will be transformed as only Jesus can do. Many churches are concerned about the cost of ministries that reach out to others, and for most churches internet evangelism is free because people who could become internet missionaries already have internet access. We need to equip and send them.

Care

The web is usually not the right place to address serious care issues such as counseling and support groups. These are best done in person, but web empowering these ministries allows more time for face-to-face ministry by taking care of time-consuming details on the web. You can use the church website to provide basic support to care ministries by including care-related resources such as online teaching, contact information for support organizations, and dates and times for various care-related events. Use your website to list meeting information for local support groups. Also, for less severe cases, a private online forum or email list can enable a support group to stay in contact and its members to keep one another accountable between face-to-face meetings.

Missions

Since mission activities usually occur at a distance from a church, people in the church may not fully understand or relate to missions. The web can make the connection by helping people in the church understand missions and helping missionaries feel a closer relationship with the people who support them.

We were surprised by the number of missionaries who have computers and internet access. Even if missionaries do not have internet access, include a page on the church website for introducing visitors to the missionaries and missions that the church supports. Photos and maps are valuable communicators. Be sure to obtain missionaries' permission before adding them to the page; sometimes inclusion could expose them to dangerous or awkward situations. If missionaries have internet access and it is safe to include them, they can also post news or a periodic newsletter on the missions page.

Missionaries who would like more communication and interactivity might find a blog helpful. By using a blog, missionaries can keep the church up-to-date in a less formal and more personal way. Visitors can comment on the blog to communicate with the missionary. For missionaries who prefer to write less frequently or are in locations that would make blogging on the public internet unwise, create a missionary prayer page where only missionaries can post. We have done this, and the missionaries appreciated it. People from the church who want to support missions can subscribe to receive the missionaries' prayer requests via email. Missionaries say that they like being able to post a prayer request, knowing that people in the church will be praying for it soon afterward because sometimes missionary prayer needs are urgent. Missionaries in more dangerous environments appreciate the protection provided by the anonymous post capability. They can still post prayer requests, but the general public does not need to know who or where they are.

If you'd like to try something interesting and fun, schedule a live chat with a missionary who has a reliable internet connection. You can even hold the chat session during a meeting about missions. Or the group can talk to the missionary via Skype audio or video, depending on what the internet connections can deliver. If possible, you can display live video of the missionary on a large screen. I use Skype for conducting live video training to groups thousands of miles away. It is easy to set up, and I get to just sit in my living room and talk to them. I am amazed at how well this works, and it is free.

Internet tools can make mission trips come alive for the people back home. You can promote mission trips on the church website, and visitors can sign up to participate in a mission trip. If the mission team has access to the internet during the trip, they can create a mission trip blog to document each day of the trip. If cell phones work where they are, they can use Twitter to send frequent messages to everyone back home who is interested, and the stream of Twitter messages can be posted on the church website. Twitter is nice because messages can be sent more frequently without the need for a computer with internet access. This allows people back home to follow the status of each day's activities and pray for current requests, such as someone who has become ill or if transportation has broken down. Family and friends really appreciate the updates and feel more part of the trip. Recently, our church was involved in a massive community-service project, and we had a roaming Twitter reporter who "live-tweeted" the event. It was kind of fun for those of us getting our hands dirty to see our efforts being tweeted about.

A mission trip photo gallery is also very popular, and TYPO3 includes several photo gallery extensions. If someone on the team has a digital camera and can upload photos during the trip, visitors monitoring the trip can view the photos right away. Sometimes the connection to the internet is good enough to support a blog but not good enough to post large photo files. In these cases, we post the photos when the team returns, and they are still a popular feature. Mission trip photos tend to be especially interesting and thought provoking.

We usually leave the blog and photos on the website long after the trip. These tools can help people who are interested in future mission trips to understand what their trip may be like.

Hospitality

One of the greatest barriers keeping new visitors from coming to a church is that they do not know what to expect. A website can give a new visitor the opportunity to learn about a church without the stress and time associated with an actual visit. One powerful feature to extend hospitality is a virtual tour that allows people to go through the steps of visiting the church and to learn what will happen along the way. The tour should include practical steps that most visitors are concerned about, like where to park, where to enter the church, where to enter if using a wheelchair, where to take kids of different ages, how kids will be signed in, how parents will be contacted if their kids need them, what to wear, where the restrooms are, what the seating options are, what first-time visitors are asked to do, where assistance can be found, what some of the people they are likely to meet will look like, what the worship style will be, and so on. I would love a feature like this if I were looking for a new church.

A virtual tour does not require fancy technology. You can implement it with a straightforward series of webpages. Instructions and pictures, including maps of the area and of the inside of the church, are helpful, too. Knowing how to create video or Flash is beneficial, but the information is what is most important. Some churches include a 360-degree virtual experience of their sanctuaries. Although this is fun, it is typically expensive to have done and shows only one room from one central point. I do not recommend doing this unless you want one simply because it is interesting.

Ministry Teams

With people's busy schedules, it often becomes difficult for ministry teams to meet in person. Two internet tools are helpful for many different teams in the church. First, private forums or email lists are handy for functions like keeping in touch, asking individuals to do certain tasks, reporting the status of current activities, planning events, sharing prayer requests, and teaching. Second, for ministries that need to exchange files within the team, a private file-sharing tool is useful. Private file sharing allows common files to be both exchanged and archived.

For groups—the church staff, main church leaders, administrative boards, and church members—an intranet may also be a valuable tool. An intranet is a private set of webpages accessible only to members of the group. It could include training, policy information, forms, lists of members, a forum, minutes from meetings, and a calendar. If you implement an intranet, make plans for keeping the list of members up-to-date to ensure that the correct people have access and unauthorized people do not.

Newsletters

Many churches use monthly or quarterly newsletters to communicate with attendees. Newsletters are important communication tools, but paper versions are costly to produce and mail. An electronic version has several advantages over paper. You can make an online newsletter longer and more colorful because, unlike with paper and ink, webpages with color do not cost extra. As I like to remind my friends who are print designers, our pictures can move and talk—online newsletters can include audio and video. (Of course, if you still have need for a number of printed newsletters, you can always create a printable version as well.) You can send online newsletters out more frequently and can therefore include more timely information. If you keep it fairly short, you can send an online newsletter every week at a specific day and time and be very effective. One newsletter per week is probably enough for most people to receive in their email inbox.

There are three types of delivery mechanisms for online newsletters:

1. Post the newsletter contents on the church website. This allows you to create a full-featured newsletter that includes various web features.
2. Send the contents via email. One challenge with email is that different email programs often display HTML email differently, so limit email newsletters to simple HTML features. One advantage of email is that it comes to the visitor's computer without the visitor having to take any additional action.
3. Combine the first two options: post the majority of the newsletter on the website, but send a starter email to all subscribers. This option has the advantages of the other two options. The starter email should be a simple HTML email that will display correctly using most email software. It should contain the theme of the newsletter, titles of the online contents, and many links to the website. Some of the links should go to new information, but others should go to commonly used features of the site. The newsletter notifies website visitors of new content and promotes the website by reminding visitors of various features and getting them accustomed to going to the website for information.

TYPO3 includes an extension that supports the process of creating an online newsletter and then sending that newsletter to a list of subscribers on a periodic basis. On the Web-Empowered Church website, we have this installed. The real power is that it can automatically incorporate content from around the WEC website into the newsletter. It can do this because the newsletter is generated from a webpage. The WEC newsletter automatically includes our last four blog entries and a live count of the total number of users registered on the WEC website. At the appropriate time the newsletter page is processed to create the HTML email, which it then sends out to the subscribers at he scheduled date and time.

With any email sent from the web server, there is the possibility that subscriber spam services may block the email. (Spam filters are programs that run on a mail server or on a visitor's local computer and attempt to determine whether or not each email is unwanted advertising or some other unsolicited email.) Spam filters have many setup options, but if a filter suspects an email is spam, it will usually move the email to a special folder. The subscriber may never see that email. As you create the template for your starter email, test spam filters by sending the email to different email accounts. The rules for getting email through spam filters change as spammers develop new techniques and spam filters counter them. You may want to test more often, or you may want to switch to a very simple email. In addition, encourage subscribers to whitelist your email address. (Whitelisting tells the spam filter software to allow emails from the specified email address to pass through the spam filter without being checked.) Some visitors do not have access to their spam whitelist, and many visitors may not know how to make this change; however, those who are successful will receive your emails. To further complicate the issue, many countries have antispam laws that vary and change and that may affect the bulk email you send.

In every bulk email, you should include instructions and a link to help people unsubscribe from the email list. Also include the name, mailing address, and phone number for your organization at the bottom of each email. This is desirable internet etiquette. Your email is clearly not spam, but these two items are commonly requested within antispam laws and help identify that your email is not spam. As you begin to send many emails at a time, you will need to ensure that the email is fully compliant with the latest spam laws and guidelines. Copies of the spam laws from around the world can be found at SpamLaws.com. Some larger internet providers may have additional rules to follow for multiple emails sent to their subscribers, and they can block all emails from your domain if they suspect you are sending spam.

Leader Communications

Newsletters are a common way for leaders to communicate with those they serve; however, for more direct communications, a leader may want to use a blog. A pastor's blog is included by default in the initial installation of the WEC-TYPO3 software. If a pastor's blog is created, it is important that the pastor knows how to blog and is committed to keeping the blog updated. A blog can become a burden to a pastor unless the pastor naturally likes to write. Another leadership empowerment tool is a group chat with a ministry leader. If you use group chat, it may be easier to have a fast typist support the leader so the leader has more time to think without needing to type. A group chat is especially useful when there is a special issue to discuss, such as a church building project. If the chat conversation would be of interest to others, be sure to post a transcript of the conversation on your website.

Events

Events of all kinds (worship, classes, mission trips, concerts, and so on) are an important part of church life. You can announce and describe events on the website, and you can also place them on an online calendar. As the calendar grows, it is beneficial to use a calendar that can be limited to display only events in specific categories defined by each visitor. For example, if a visitor has no children, he or she may prefer not to see youth events on the calendar. Another popular calendar feature is the ability to copy events from the online church calendar to a local calendar on the visitor's computer. For example, the events on the church calendar can be automatically inserted into a visitor's Microsoft Outlook calendar and loaded onto a handheld device like a smart phone.

Online event registration is also valuable. This feature includes web forms that collect the needed information and send it to the appropriate person via email, store it in a database, or both. More powerful event registration applications can perform functions like limiting registrations to a specified total number, providing rosters of registrants for events, and archiving information on who attended which event.

The most technically challenging feature to support event registration is online sales. Sales include purchasing products, like a book needed for a course of study, or paying a fee for participating in a conference. Online-store software is fairly common; however, online stores are typically more difficult to set up than other web features. There are multiple open-source online stores that could be used.

The two biggest challenges when setting up an online store are purchasing a Secure Sockets Layer (SSL) certificate and installing it, and getting a merchant account and setting up the software to use it. You must purchase the SSL certificate through a process that includes verifying your organization's identity. The certificate is actually just a long list of numbers used to identify your website and to enable it to securely exchange private information (like credit card numbers) over the internet. The merchant account enables one to process credit cards and other electronic forms of exchanging money. A merchant account connects to your church's bank account to transfer funds to and from that account. A merchant account costs money, and each online transaction costs money.

There are companies that offer solutions to simplify the store setup process. Some offer preconfigured online stores like Yahoo!

Small Business or Vendio.com, and some offer only transaction processing like PayPal and Authorize.net. These solutions usually take visitors to another website to make the purchase. Your hosting company may also offer support for online stores. Any of these may be viable solutions for your organization; however, providing a full online store locally on your website offers the best and most intuitive experience for a visitor making a purchase.

Stewardship

The dilemma of accepting online giving is that most online purchases are done using credit cards and most people do not pay off their credit cards each month, so online giving may promote debt, which is not typically something we want to promote. One possible solution is to support only those methods of online payment that do not involve credit such as e-checks or debit cards, but these may be more difficult to set up and to enforce.

If you have an online store, you can take donations online by setting up a donation product. With proper security measures (such as SSL) in place, there are opportunities for managing the church finances online and for tracking giving. Allowing visitors access to a summary of all of their tithes, offerings, and items they have donated is a useful feature to complement online giving. This, too, can be challenging, but useful, to implement.

If you do not have an online store, you may want to use a donation processing company such as Egiving Systems (egiv ingsystems.org). Using such a company may be a good solution because it greatly simplifies the implementation, and it adds features specific to donations such as automatic monthly giving and electronic checks.

Fellowship

Online fellowship and community happen when people connect online. As churches become more web empowered, many of the website features will enhance fellowship and community. A set of forums where people can gather and communicate is valuable. You can create a few forums that represent common interests for your organization. We have a forum simply called "fellowship" where people from the church can talk about any healthy subject they choose. This forum works well, and the title of the forum encourages healthy connections.

E-cards are another way to connect people to people. E-cards are personal electronic greeting cards. Like traditional greeting cards, they are available for many categories, such as birthdays, weddings, anniversaries, sympathy, encouragement, and more. You can also use them to invite people to church or to special events such as Christmas, Easter, or a festival. We created our e-cards using Flash. A visitor who wants to send an e-card selects a card, fills in the destination name and email address, enters a personal message for the inside of the card, previews the card online, and then sends the card. The person receiving the card receives a notification via an email, which contains a unique link that takes him or her back to the website to view the card. Hosting the e-card on the website helps ensure that the e-card displays and works correctly. With Flash, the cards can include sound, animation, video, and links.

Small Groups

A website can empower small-group (also called "cell-group") ministry by connecting visitors with existing groups in the church. An easy way to do this is to provide an email form that collects information to help match visitors to small groups. A person who knows the available small groups well reviews the email contents, identifies appropriate small groups, and contacts the visitor with specific suggestions. Another option is to include information on the website such as when and where groups meet, the main focus of each group, the ages and family situations of group members, and the contact information for the leaders. A visitor can contact a group leader via email or a web form. However, to protect the leaders' privacy, do not provide their addresses, phone numbers, or personal emails on the website; instead, implement email aliases that forward to personal email addresses. For example, an email address such as SouthFamilyGroup@yourchurch.org could forward to the personal email address of the leader of the South family small group. A web application can also enable small-group leaders to provide membership and attendance information to the church.

There are many opportunities for enhancing small groups once they are established. Examples include a private forum, a calendar, a photo gallery, a list of news and announcements, a prayer list, and more. As long as you keep the information private and accessible only within the group, and as long as you have permission, group members can share personal information. The private small-group area could include addresses, phone numbers, birthdays, and anniversaries. This brings the group closer and keeps them connected between meetings. Free social networking websites can be ideal for a small-group website because they can be set to private for members only, have many features a group could use, and be self-created easily by most anyone without the web team needing to set them up.

Memorials

For hundreds of years, churches have provided memorials for people who have gone to be with the Lord. Traditionally, memorials have been in the form of long-lasting items such as stones, plaques, or trees. Online memorials are a unique way to continue the tradition. I credit Leonard Sweet with this concept. We have tried it at Ginghamsburg, and it has worked. In general, people think online memorials are a good idea, but for some, it is a bit too different to consider, especially in a time of grieving. Given the features that the web can provide and the fact that people can access the memorial from anywhere on the internet,

I expect these to become more popular in churches. Currently, this feature is most frequently offered by funeral homes.

Online memorials can include many different features. The memorials at Ginghamsburg include a main photo and a short life story, with options for a photo gallery, a video, and a reflections page. The reflections page can allow visitors to post comments and thoughts whenever they would like to post them. The church has agreed to host the online memorials for as long as the technology allows.

CHAPTER 13

Looking Toward the Future

Visions of internet ministry and the Web-Empowered Church

The world is becoming increasingly connected, initially through computers and wired connections, but now through wireless connections and other devices. Everything is connecting to the internet—houses, cars, televisions, video recorders, cameras, watches, appliances, and more. The increasingly ubiquitous internet connectivity and worldwide connectedness provide many new ministry opportunities for our web-empowered ministries. We just need to be ready for them.

In time, all ministries will include a web component of some kind, and we won't think much about it. Internet technology will support our day-to-day operations and will provide the bidirectional communication mechanisms necessary to deliver ministries to the people we serve as well as to evangelize non-Christians around the world. The internet will allow us to connect with and to become more integrated into people's lives according to their specific needs. Handheld devices, like smart phones and tablets, will enable the church to be connected and available 24/7 to those it serves without leaving users feeling intruded upon. Automatic customization will filter the content that is sent to users and displayed on the website to tailor it to each individual's needs and interests. Single people will see an announcement for a singles gathering, but not an announcement for a married couples event.

Live worship will include an electronic bulletin for people's smart phones or tablets that provides all the information for the event, including notes and words to songs, as well as the ability to provide live feedback to the pastor and worship team. Online worship events will also be available during the week and will offer a full worship experience. Christian education, like university education, is migrating to more online classes. Some classes will be purely self-paced, and others will be taken with a group and include online discussion and exchange with others in the class. As churches partner together, large selections of online classes will be available to anyone who wants to learn and grow in Christ. By logging in, users can give and review their financial giving, update personal information, set preferences, sign up for events, and more.

On the mission field, we will get live messages from mission teams and will watch live video and speak with missionaries across the world. Daily devotions will be available in text or audio on handheld devices or computers. Connectivity with the church will be just a tap away on a handheld device with opportunities available for listing and registering for events, watching or listening to sermons, viewing and posting prayer requests, and more. The message, the mission, and the people remain the same, but we will adapt to the changing ways in which the content is packaged, delivered, and received, and we will be able to reach more people and to meet the specific needs of the people we serve. We will use technology to minister better. These are technology trends that are happening now and will happen in other areas of life as well; it is up to us to be there, too, and maybe even lead the way.

Web-empowering your church or organization is not easy, just as most significant ministry is not easy. But you are not alone. The Web-Empowered Church (WEC) ministry and growing community of Web-Empowered Church servants from around the world are available to assist you. This community is part of a movement of God. WEC is not pushing you toward a specific

Christian theology or type of church. WEC wants to empower you to do your Christian ministry in your unique way. If you prefer not to use our tools, you can still be part of this movement by web-empowering your ministries.

Tools to Make It Happen from Web-Empowered Church

The WEC movement is made of God's people in churches and Christian organizations around the world partnering together to help apply internet technology to increase the impact of the church. The WEC ministry has developed and continues to develop powerful web-based ministry-enhancing tools to empower ministries now and to prepare for increasing impact in the future. This WEC software is used by churches and Christian organizations around the world. The mission of WEC is to innovatively apply *web* technology to *empower* the worldwide *church* for ministry. WEC is a ministry of Christian Technology Ministries International (CTMI), a nonprofit 501(c)(3) organization committed to advancing computer and communications technology in the church to enhance the work of Jesus Christ in the world.

If this sounds exciting to you, please consider joining other Christians around the world to help expand WEC's reach and to get WEC capabilities into churches and ministries. The WEC ministry also seeks dedicated Christians with technology skills and passion to help develop and deploy technology, and donors who share our vision and want to help fuel this world-changing movement. Please use the free ministry tools and resources provided by WEC at WebEmpoweredChurch.org. We've created powerful ministry tools, but they will not fulfill their ministry purposes until they are deployed on church and ministry websites like yours. Besides this book and WEC's free website software, WEC's website includes free online training and community support forums with participants from web-empowered organizations around the world. And if you need extra assistance, WEC also offers a full line of services including helping you plan to web empower your organization, moving content to a WEC-based website, developing websites, customizing template design, hosting websites, and developing custom features. WEC offers these services to help speed the process for your organization to become web empowered.

The main software WEC provides is called the WEC Starter Package. This free and open-source software immediately gives you a fully functional ministry website with many powerful web-empowering ministry features to support sermons, devotions, online teaching, Scripture display, maps, prayer, volunteer matching, calendaring, audio and video playing, blogging, social networking connection, online worship, and more. These features can be disabled also and enabled when you are ready to use them. In addition, WEC has custom applications that enable your visitors to view and interact with your website using a handheld device. WEC also includes a number of customizable and professionally designed templates that you can choose from to provide a quality look and feel for your website. To learn more about the latest features of the WEC Starter Package, please visit demo.WebEmpoweredChurch.org to see a live example of the latest version of the WEC Starter Package. The demonstration website also includes a template selector that allows you to view the website with any of the available templates.

Conclusion

Thank you for your willingness to serve in this exciting and unique ministry. I hope and pray that this book supports and encourages you on your unique journey in internet ministry. Please remember that this is not easy, but the impact you can have on people's lives can be huge and can help change the world for Jesus Christ. May God bless you, your family, and your ministry. Please send me an email (mark@webempowered church.org) when you get your website online. Such success stories are always a blessing to me and the Web-Empowered Church Team.

I am praying for each and every one of you as you work to web empower your church or Christian organization.

Heavenly Father, Creator and Redeemer, we pray for those of us in the Web-Empowered Church movement as we seek to empower our churches and Christian organizations for ministry using internet technology. This is a new and difficult challenge that needs your guidance and wisdom to succeed. Help the Christian community welcome our ministry with open arms; and help leaders embrace technology as a tool for ministry. Help us use the web to expand evangelism, discipleship, and care throughout the world. And when the magnitude of the challenge feels bigger than we are, please help us to rely on you and to boldly step forward to do your will to the best of our abilities. Please protect and bless the efforts of the Web-Empowered Church community of researchers, developers, testers, trainers, and users around the world. We are your servants and are blessed to serve you in internet ministry. In Jesus' name. Amen.

Mark's List of Essential CyberTips

Over the years as we have developed and maintained our website, I have compiled a list of "CyberTips." Almost all these tips are the direct result of lessons learned. My hope is that this list will help you experience fewer of these lessons. Most of these tips were mentioned somewhere in this book. They are repeated here, in no particular order, for your convenience and reference.

1. Value the people on your team more than the task of building your website.
2. Start with static content first, and add changing content only as you are able to keep it up-to-date.
3. Don't post personal phone numbers or addresses without permission.
4. Never post private email addresses; instead, create email aliases.
5. Don't violate copyright laws, and especially watch out for copyrighted music.
6. Design for people with low-end PCs, modems, and standard 1024 x 768 display resolution monitors.
7. Keep the total page size with graphics under 150 kilobytes.
8. Use a common CSS file that can be cached by the browser.
9. Don't use HTML frames.
10. Limit the page content width to 985 pixels.
11. Don't use graphical backgrounds; white or black is usually best.
12. Don't make pages longer than three screens vertically.

13. Never require horizontal scrolling.
14. Keep the link colors the same throughout the website, and use an obvious color.
15. Never underline text that is not a link because it will look like a link.
16. Use animation sparingly and purposefully; slower and smoother animation is more user friendly.
17. Never allow banner advertisements on a ministry website.
18. Include many photos of people.
19. Get written permission to post photos.
20. Put a logo or photos of people on the home page instead of a photo of your building.
21. Put the organization's address in the page footer.
22. Never put the words "under construction" or a construction graphic anywhere on your website. The page should simply remain hidden until complete.
23. Provide an alternative to using the back button in your navigation.
24. Use a CMS, and train many people to help maintain your website.
25. Let capable and trustworthy people who generate the content enter the content when possible.
26. Make sure photos are resized to their final display size, not just resized with HTML (a CMS should take care of that).
27. Use JPGs for photos.
28. Use GIFs for animation and cartoons.
29. Support visitors using PDAs and smart phones.
30. Transcribe your sermons and post them in text format if possible.
31. Minimize use of plug-ins and technology tricks.
32. Avoid Java applets and ActiveX.
33. Add interactive features and online community to your website.

34. Don't do internet ministry alone; get at least a few other people to help.
35. Make nasty or inappropriate posts to your website into ministry opportunities.
36. Use fewer words; use words most people understand; remember that visitors may be from far away.
37. Narrow the columns to less than 500 pixels wide to make large blocks of text more readable.
38. Avoid mistakes, and make removing mistakes top priority.
39. Know from the start that creating webpages takes much longer than you would ever think.
40. Take security very seriously.
41. Remember that creating a website for your organization is not about technology; it is about ministry.
42. Use standard XHTML and validate it.
43. Plan your folder structure, folder names, file naming, and styles.
44. Use Flash or video to communicate information, not just for how it looks.
45. Don't use Flash for navigation.
46. Design for accessibility for persons who are visually and hearing impaired.
47. Laugh at yourself when you mess up.
48. Avoid using free online services that include ads; if you do use these services, be sure to monitor them.
49. Encrypt all posted email addresses so spam spider programs can't get them.
50. Don't use anything from another website without asking permission.
51. Feel free to link to other websites without asking for permission.
52. Be very careful what sites you link to because people consider your links to be endorsements.

53. Do not assume that you can legally post certain music on the web just because you legally used it in church. It may require two separate permissions.
54. Try to have complete information but know that missing information is better than wrong information on the website.
55. Provide an obvious way to contact the web team from the website to send suggestions and questions.
56. Limit use of PDF documents that need to be printed and complex documents that few people will read online.
57. Pray a lot for this ministry.
58. Don't add a large set of links to other websites on a links page unless there are special reasons why your visitors need them.
59. Do not allow music or video to automatically begin playing on a page unless a visitor requests it by clicking a link.
60. Know that your website will go down; computers will fail; networks will fail.
61. Test your templates and unique pages with multiple browsers.
62. Link to a mapping website for a map to your church, but don't copy the map because that is a copyright violation.
63. Include the Global Positioning System (GPS) coordinates along with other church location information.
64. Never add a visitor counter to a webpage; you can find out how many visitors you have from the web server logs and other analytics services.
65. Consider a copyright notice on your pages. It is not required in order to protect them; it is just a reminder to visitors.
66. Keep things simple, especially for any actions visitors may need to take.
67. Don't add a calendar if you are not able to keep it complete and up-to-date.

68. Try to limit each visitor to only one username and password if there are features that require a logon.
69. Give visitors the option of playing media immediately via progressive download or downloading it to play later.
70. Remember that free online services can be powerful ministry tools to connect to the world but they may not always be safe places.

Finally, here are a few reminders to help keep you smiling even when computers are being difficult:

1. If you think you understand computers, sit back and enjoy the brief moment.
2. Computers are here to humble us, not to help us.
3. Computers do what the programmer tells them to do, not what the programmer wants them to do.